ELIZABETH WETTLAUFER THE KILLER NURSE

First edition. July 14, 2021.

Copyright © 2021 Pete Dover.

ISBN: 979-8215011737

Written by Pete Dover.

ELIZABETH WETTLAUFER The Killer Nurse

PETE DOVER

A Nurse from Our Nightmares – The Murderous Reign of Elizabeth Wettlaufer

There is something of the Kathy Bates about Elizabeth Wettlaufer. The great actresses' portrayal of Annie Wilkes in 'Misery' evokes a sense of similarity with photographs of the nurse from Ontario, handcuffed and looking strangely empty. Perhaps it is the hair, straight and of a style almost, but not quite, every day. Or it could be the slightly dumpy looks, creating a face that is pasty and unhealthy. Most likely it is the eyes – the windows on a mind where the view is too often one of the darkest, emptiest night.

Annie was, of course, famously a nurse; one who had a habit of sending her patients – elderly and weak – off to an early grave. She'd experienced a tough upbringing and a failed romance. She was a loner, one who was forced to enjoy her own company due to the absence of any other.

We don't know if, like Annie Wilkes, Elizabeth Wettlaufer has a favourite author. One who (if chance should present itself) she would bring home from some accident or catastrophe, surround with stifling love and ensure he stayed with her, dependent and compliant, in order to finish his 'greatest novel'. An undertaking which would naturally be dedicated to his somewhat unwanted angel of mercy. But one thing we do know is that the similarities between Stephen King's fictional murderess and the real life Canadian who dispatched at least eight elderly patients to an early death go beyond just the physical similarities they shared.

In fact, Wettlaufer fancied herself as a bit of a literary queen. She published her own poetry online, writing under the name of Betty Weston. One contained the following lines:

> *'She watches some life drain*
> *From the notch in his neck vein.*
> *As it soothingly pools*
> *It smothers her pain.'*

Given the crimes she would go on to commit, those lines must be read with some trepidation.

Elizabeth's criminal career began while she worked at the Caressant Care home in Woodstock, Ontario. Located handily in the middle of town, the long-term care facility had manufactured a good reputation locally. Indeed, right up until Elizabeth confessed to her serial killings, few had an inkling that something was very wrong with the nursing and retirement home. Or, indeed, that the helpful little night nurse who circulated with her clinking trolley of medications kept a very dark secret behind her smiling façade.

Elizabeth Mae Parker was born on June 10th, 1967. Later, she added Tracey as an additional middle name, and an 'e' to the short-form Beth. While those changing times around her birth might have been right in the heart of the high jinks of the swinging sixties, life at home for Bethe was no free and easy jaunt. She was brought up in a strict Baptist home, under a restrictive regime led by her father.

Yet although her father was strict and unbending, the family were close. As Elizabeth grew up a strong bond developed between her and both of her parents. Outside the home, though, life was more challenging. As a girl, she might appear to be diminutive in size, but not in personality. Yet appearances can be misleading. The small and chubby kid might seem to bubble with enthusiasm, but in truth school was an ordeal. She played goalkeeper for the field hockey team and was a trombonist in the school band. But the fit for her was forced. 'She was often the odd kid out,' remembers her neighbor and childhood friend Glyn Hart. 'She was shy and awkward a lot.' Still, Bethe at least tried to fit in. It was just that she didn't know how to do so.

Perhaps a reason for this was that her home life, which she shared as a child with her brother, was stiflingly religious. Added to this, as adolescence beckoned, sexuality became an issue for her. Bethe was a lesbian, or at least held tendencies in that direction. Some unsubstantiated reports talk of dabblings with other girls at High School during her school years. Such adolescent experiments are hardly unusual, however.

Yet her parents, her father in particular, believed homosexuality to be a sin, and Bethe was driven away from her sexuality. While once again unsubstantiated, some of the blogs and accounts that naturally grow up around a sensational court case such as hers suggest that she was even sent on a camp to be 'cured' of her lesbianism during those crucial formative years. The jigsaw that makes up a person's life is created from numerous small, but important, pieces.

While many of the assertions about Elizabeth Wettlaufer are just speculation, what is more certain is that Bethe considered herself a lesbian, and somehow saw that as something wrong. The confusion her nature provoked promoted feelings that haunted her well into adult life. One day, with a joy bordering on the unstable, she announced to friends in her tenement block that she 'found God and wasn't a lesbian anymore.'

The former nurse also suffered from drug addiction. Twice she went into rehab to conquer her condition, which she claimed was fueled by the medications on the drugs trolley in the nursing home in which she worked. Such was the nature of her role that she had access to these drugs without supervision.

When she was a child, however hard life was, Bethe seemed a girl who was determined to make the most of her lot. After High School she earned a diploma in Religious Studies, taken at a bible college, then took a qualification at nursing school. By 1995 she was a licensed registered nurse.

By the time she had established herself at Caressant Care, she was moving up the ladder and earning close to $60000 per year. A part of that was because she was more than happy to work night shifts. More than happy. Soon, a byzantine, troubled personality would seize the opportunity working nights presented and begin a killing spree that would turn her into one of Canada's most prolific serial killers.

However, while it is undoubtedly the case that Bethe suffered from multiple mental health issues, she was far from an innocent victim whose actions were beyond her control.

'She'd have temper tantrums if things didn't go her own way,' observed one former colleague.

Her attitude towards her victims was complex as well. She seemed to hold an illogical anger towards her male targetss, seeing in them aggressiveness and inappropriate behavior which she felt deserved punishment. 'His time was up,' she later said of the first man she killed. For the women, she claimed that she was acting in their best interests, in her mind putting them out of their 'Wettlaufer' defined misery. To her they were simply pets put down by an owner who means well but is uninformed about animal welfare. Fundamentally, Elizabeth Wettlaufer liked to play God. Both the one of the New Testament, and the one of the Old.

'She disclosed that it wasn't accidental,' said Glyn Hart, 'and then she disclosed that it wasn't just one.'

Indeed, it was not.

Yet what seems painfully apparent is that had Bethe not confessed to her crimes, they would not have been discovered. At her subsequent trial Wettlaufer was sentenced to a twenty-five-year term, without the possibility of parole. Yet had she kept her story to herself, she would still most likely be free and practicing today.

An enquiry reached this conclusion, having looked in detail at all matters surrounding the murders, along with at least six failed attempts to kill other residents of the homes in which she worked. Commissioner Eileen E Gillese said: 'The evidence showed that no one suspected that Wettlaufer was intentionally harming those under her care – not the residents of their families. Not those who worked alongside Wettlaufer, and not those who managed and supervised her.'

The commissioner also pointed out that as a senior nurse, Elizabeth was under the 'indirect oversight' of the Ministry of Health and Long-Term Care, which was responsible for inspecting the kind of institutions at which she worked. Coroners had also investigated the deaths of some of the seniors who became her victims. Not one of the individuals working at these offices suspected foul play had taken place.

Whether Bethe confessed to her crimes in an effort to stop is not clear. Certainly, she later told friends of the guilt she felt for her actions. She had given up her job in London, Ontario and enrolled for treatment in the Toronto Centre for Addiction and Mental Health. It was while she was there that she confessed to a psychiatrist that she was, in fact, a serial killer. He was not the first to hear Bethe's confessions. A lawyer had earlier advised her to keep her news secret. However, following the report of the psychiatrist made to the police, Bethe took matters into her own hands, emailing the College of Nurses of Ontario to resign her position as a registered nurse. She had 'deliberately harmed patients...and was being investigated by police,' she said in an email to the organization. Her resignation was a case of too little much too late as far as her victims and their families were concerned.

While police decided whether to charge the 49-year-old nurse on eight counts of homicide, she was required to sign a peace bond which placed her under curfew and banned her from providing any form of health care.

Already struggling, despite her good salary, to pay her rent, she was forced to move out of her two bedroomed apartment and head back home to her parents. Yet for all her troubles, to neighbors it seemed as though Elizabeth Wettlaufer could not come to terms with the seriousness of her situation. An anonymous neighbor spoke to the Canadian newspaper, The Star.

This neighbor told the paper that Bethe has asked her what residents of the block were saying about her. The neighbor replied that there were suspicions she had killed someone. The former nurse's reaction was hardly what might have been expected under such circumstances. 'And she starts laughing her head off. She was hysterical. She thought the whole thing was funny,' reported the female neighbor.

Another neighbor, Nancy Gilbert, explained how the odd little nurse was frighteningly open – indiscreet perhaps – about her drug problem. She was quite prepared to tell Gilbert that she took the drugs to which she was becoming addicted from the medical cart she ran at the nursing home. 'She said she got to the point where she didn't want it to control her life or her job,' said Gilbert, referring to Wettlaufer's first of two spells in rehab.

A note on Facebook written by Bethe herself perhaps offered a further insight into the instability in her mind. This was recorded in October 2015 and refers to her own battles with addiction. 'My own voice called me in the darkness,' she wrote, employing somewhat dramatic language, 'Other hands lifted me when I chose the light. One year ago, today I woke up not dead. 365 days clean and sober.'

But despite the rather flowery method of expression, once more we see the strong side of Bethe coming through. The one that coped at school with being the outsider. The one determined to see through what she wanted. Battling addiction is no walk in the park. Perhaps she deserved her moment of self-congratulation. Sad that she could only share it with the hidden friends of the Facebook community.

The drugs had already carried a cost for her, at least according to the story she told other neighbors. It seems as though, in 2014, her reliance on these chemicals had led to a terrible accident. She issued the wrong medication to a patient while she was, in her own words, 'fried'. That led to her leaving Caressant Care. 'She wasn't fired. They said if she left quietly, they would just let it go,' explained one neighbor.

The story makes sense. Addiction is considered a health condition in Canada and not a ground upon which a worker, even one as responsible as a nurse, can easily be fired. The Ontario Human Rights Tribunal had recently decreed that addiction was a disability. A case had arisen before it involving a nurse, and the tribunal had decided that she could not be fired as a result of behavior emerging from her addiction.

Caressant may well have faced an expensive labor dispute had they sought to dismiss Wettlaufer from her role, even though her error was serious, and committed while under the influence of drugs. Further, the institution was a for-profit organization. Reputation was important to it. It did not wish to become involved in a lengthy court battle.

There could have been some darker reasons for this reluctance as well. Despite the fine presentation of the institution it successfully portrayed, under the surface matters were not as smooth as they might appear. During the night shift, according to people who worked at the nursing home, staffing was often inadequate. Many of the care assistants worked other jobs, and absenteeism was high. On those occasions when staff were unexpectedly absent, the management was reluctant to meet the cost of overtime or substitute workers.

Ross Gerrie was an official of the union which represented a number of staff at Caressant Care. 'There is no legislation that requires a certain number of minimum hours of care per patient, so the home piles the work on to the next person,' he said. 'The problem is industry wide.'

Certainly, if any member of staff – especially a senior one such as Bethe – wished to exploit the system, it was easy to do so.

There is yet another possible reason for Caressant Care not wishing to become embroiled in a lengthy case over a member of staff's indiscretion. Although most of its Ministry of Health and Long-Term Care inspection reports are good, this was not always the case. Two inspections from 2014 and 2015 raised the sorts of concerns which could seriously damage its reputation...and therefore its profit line.

'In resident bathrooms...a wall visibly stained with urine, brown/yellow substance around the base of the toilets. 'noted a 2015 report, going on to list other hygiene concerns.

Perhaps the decision to reach a mutually agreed termination of contract with its employee was the best route for Caressant. Certainly, official bodies note the difficulty of firing someone for the reason of substance abuse:

'When a nurse is suspected of substance abuse or stealing meds and investigation is initiated,' explained a senior care official from the College of Nurses of Ontario. 'it is very hard to prove it and it takes quite a bit of time.'

Nevertheless, when, a couple of years later, Elizabeth Wettlaufer's crimes became known, and she was arrested, three senior managers were fired.

For a nurse of Bethe's experience, it was not too difficult to get another job after leaving Caressant care. She was next employed by Meadow Park nursing home, which is in the nearby town of London.

It was not just experience that helped her to find alternative employment quickly. Because, in some ways, Bethe was a good nurse. She was well liked by staff and residents. She was kind. The home in Woodstock had a policy, astonishingly, of limiting residents to three incontinence pads per day. Bethe was always happy to provide as many as were needed, even when it meant breaking house rules.

She was known for being willing to step in and help others. One co-worker refused to be named, out of fear that she would be fired by the home (which, we might conclude, says a lot) but was happy to describe working with Bethe in return for anonymity.

'She was great with the residents. I've never seen her not be nice to anybody,' she said.

It seems as though Wettlaufer began her career as a murderer in late 2007, and at one stage she killed three elderly residents in a twenty-four-day period. Her means of operation was to inject insulin into her victims.

As methods of murder go, insulin is a good choice. It is hard to identify in an autopsy. Tests find it virtually impossible to distinguish between natural insulin produced by the body and the artificial substance used to control levels in diabetics and the elderly.

While it is very hard to kill using insulin by accident - a large dose is needed - death can occur very quickly, or after a number of days. This makes identifying the insulin injection as responsible practically impossible. It is a readily available drug, and not monitored in the same way as others perceived as more dangerous.

Finally, her victims were elderly. They were people already in care. Old people, sadly, do die. As devastating as each death might be to family and friends, it is not an event which causes surprise, or suspicion. As we saw earlier, it is highly unlikely that Wettlaufer would have been detected had she not confessed to her actions.

In 2007 Andrea Silcox and her family were facing up to one of the toughest decisions any grown up children can face. Their father, James, was a tough veteran of the second world war. A man who wore his medals with pride, whose views were clear and happily shared. But age was catching up. Still, he would not give in to the inevitable. 'No, I'm not using that walker,' he had boldly exclaimed when Andrea had bought matching mobility aids for her mom and dad.

But two more cruel blows hit the war time hero. The twin whammy of a stroke and developing dementia sent his well-being spiraling downhill. It was apparent that, for his own safety, he needed more care than his family could provide. It was also in 2007 that the managers of Caressant Care took on a new member of staff. A smiling, bubbly kind of nurse, whom everybody thought would help to keep elderly spirits high.

Later, James became Wettlaufer's first victim. In her confession, she described her anger at what she saw as the eighty-four-year old's inappropriate behavior. Behavior, of course, of a man with dementia. 'That evening,' she wrote, 'I got the urge to overdose James. At approximately 7.30pm I decided to overdose him with insulin, hoping he would die.'

She also said that he had called out, as he slowly passed away 'I'm sorry,' and 'I love you.' It seems fair to conclude that James Silcox was confused and was mistaking Wettlaufer for his wife.

Maurice Granat, known as Moe, had suffered from a stroke. He was 84 when he died. But incredibly Wettlaufer came closest to being caught when attacking him, just her second victim. Two of Moe's friends had arrived to see him. They had caught him fighting with Wettlaufer, and saw her inject him, telling the chums that it was medication to calm him down.

Moe died just twenty minutes later, but the associates made no connection between the injection and their friend's death. Only later did it all begin to make sense to victim's pals. 'It's spinning in my mind. I never heard before what he sounded like that day. He was struggling with her. Was he fighting her? What was going on before we'd been there?' said one of the friends.

Gladys Millard, an 87-year-old, came next and was followed by Helen Matheson. Ninety-five-year-old Helen was a former teacher, one who had started her career in a tiny, one roomed schoolhouse in rural Ontario. According to her son, Jon, she was well right up to a couple of weeks before her death. Then, she started to go down quickly, before refusing to eat. He put his mother's decline down to the ravages of old age. She died in the early hours of October 14th 2011, but it was only later that investigators revealed that Helen was also one of Elizabeth Wettlaufer's victims.

Her son had held not the slightest suspicion. 'She never complained of being mistreated at the home,' recalled Jon, 'And I always thought people were looked after fairly well. I try to think back, was there something I missed? I can't come up with anything, really. And that's the frustrating part.'

Wettlaufer's next victim was one year older than the former teacher. 96-year-old Mary Zurawainski was then followed by two more women, ninety-year-old Helen Young and Maureen Pickering, who was 79.

All were residents at the Caressant Care home. Four other confirmed victims of Wettlaufer also lived at the home, although none of these died as a direct result of the nurse's actions. Clotilde Adriano and Albina Demedeiros were sisters in their late eighties. Although both died following the insulin led attacks on them, it was decided that natural causes were responsible. Two younger men, Michael Priddle (63) and fifty-seven-year-old Wayne Hedges were also attacked at the care home.

Wettlaufer struck three more times, once with deadly consequences. Arpad Hovarth was her last murder victim, killed at the Meadow Park facility in London, Ontario. But she was also charged with 'intent to murder' seventy-seven-year-old Sandra Towler at a Paris, Ontario retirement home, and sixty-eight-year-old Beverley Bertram at her home in Ingersoll, also in Ontario.

As is so often the case when criminal activity comes to light in one of the institutions caring for our most vulnerable members of society – schools, hospitals, care homes and so forth – hindsight suddenly proves to be a wonderful asset. Commissioner Gillese made an incredible 91 recommendations in her inquiry. This is evidence of the poor standard of supervision and communication which had previously been the norm in the care industry, and particularly its for-profit arm.

And it is certainly astonishing that when Bethe left Caressant Care on a mutually agreed basis, the Woodstock based provider had no obligation to report her to any official body who may have decided to look more deeply into her case. In fact, the matter was reported to the College of Nurses of Ontario, but that organization decided that there were no 'serious concerns', even though the reason for the nurse leaving had been a serious one; that is, giving out the wrong medication. It was a decision made to look ill-judged when she became Canada's first healthcare professional to be charged with multiple murders.

Bethe was also clear that there was more than just anger behind her actions. 'I honestly thought God wanted to use me...' she claimed. 'I knew the difference between right and wrong, but I thought this was something God, or whoever, wanted me to do. But I was starting at that point to doubt that it was God.'

She also said that she felt a 'red surge' rush through her body as she was about to commit murder.

It is possible that another event, an emotionally traumatic one, played its part in her move from carer to murderer. In 1997 she had married Daniel Wettlaufer – they stayed together for a decade, but it was a childless marriage. Gradually, the two moved apart emotionally, then physically. They had been separated for just seven months when Bethe committed her first murder.

She also had another failed relationship shortly after the separation. Realizing that her real attraction was to women, she had entered into a relationship with Sheila Andrews. However, Andrews was overwhelmed by the nurse, finding her impossible to cope with.

'When she got off the plane, she almost body slammed me,' said Andrews of an early meeting between the two. 'She's just like "I've been telling everybody how much in love I am with you and we were going to get together and everything." And I'm just, like, "Whoa, slow down, sweetheart. We're just meeting." That's what kind of scared me off.'

Yet although Elizabeth held such an unstable moral compass when it came to the elderly – loving them and, at the same time, becoming so angry that she sent eight to an early grave – she did seem to show some compassion towards children. She spent a short period working at the St Elizabeth Home Health Care which included among its patients a number of children who suffered from diabetes.

She spent only six weeks working there, recognizing the temptation these potential young victims presented, and reaching the moral judgement to move away.

Elizabeth Wettlaufer is not, it seems, a person who can be judged by the same standards as most. A woman who fought against adversity, who battled to make a success of her career, who was always available to help. Yet also one mentally flawed, often unstable and prone to addiction.

Some six years before she was finally sent to prison, she wrote a poem which she published online. It will not stand the test of time and is typified by her wanton use of hyperbole. Nevertheless, 'Working Happy' is a telling piece. It gently describes of her fondness of old people. She mentions 'their wrinkles, their frailties, their refusing to eat anything but ice cream.'

She finishes by referring to the finality of their time in care, 'the resignation.'

Yet, in at least eight cases, it was Elizabeth herself who determined that her helpless victims would indeed be 'knowing this is their last home' earlier than their God intended.

MICHELLE KNOTEK

Murder is sometimes seen as a crime of the underclass; an action typified by dark, drug filled alleys or robberies gone too far. Yet one of the most shocking series of killings in American history offers an alternative view to that preconception.

Raymond, in Pacific County Washington State, is the kind of place to which most people would be happy to move. Situated on the banks of the Willapa River, close to the Pacific Ocean, it is the sort of small community that appeals to everything from families to holidaymakers to those looking for a quiet retirement town.

Then again, there are hints that Raymond's past might not be as idyllic as its location on a map of the US suggests. Firstly, interested parties should be careful when undertaking their initial research. Look up 'Raymond, Washington' and we are as likely to be directed to the page of the notorious gangster of the same name as to the riverside town.

And when we seek more information, we find that Raymond was, in its early days of the turn of the 20th Century, a somewhat wild town. It was built on boardwalks and stilts above the marshy flood plains of the river. But the rolling hills between the horseshoe shaped river and nearby ocean provided an industry to make the town wealthy – timber. Next, that income was increased as people began to learn of the hidden beauties of Washington State, and tourism grew. Good weather, its own micro-climate and abundant wildlife still attract holidaymakers from near and far. These days, the town is also the centre of the legalised marijuana industry in the region, growing and processing the plant for its homeopathic benefits.

Michelle and David Knotek lived just outside of Raymond. Their home was one of the better ones in the area – on the outside at least. Theirs was a large and beautiful farmhouse sitting in its own four acre plot. The idyll was furthered by the large number of well cared for animals that roamed the farmhouse's extensive grounds.

But inside the warm walls life was very different; three people were murdered viciously within that plot; two following months of monstrous torture after which their bodies simply stopped working. The Knotek's crimes were so vile that they were revealed to the authorities by their own daughter.

David Knotek was a worker in the construction industry who was well known and respected in the community; a local man with strong ties to the area. A Vietnam veteran, he had sought to enter the priesthood after graduating from Raymond High School in 1971. Instead of becoming a man of the cloth, however, he joined the Navy and spent five years there learning about the construction trade.

He had held down a number of other jobs in the area, including working at the town's largest employer, the Weyerhaeuser Mill. He even spent some time driving the local garbage truck.

The former mayor of Raymond, Leon Lead, summed up the way David Knotek was regarded locally: 'I've known David forever,' he said. 'He blended right in, in fact I'm surprised they (David and his wife, Michelle) are still around the area – I haven't seen him years.'

And when discussing the killings for which David had been sentenced, he went on: 'He was the last guy I would think of for something like this, a kind of Regular Joe.'

A friend from High School. John McVey gave an extra insight behind David's apparently easy going exterior. He may have been the handsome and popular guy who had a kind word for everyone, but there was a different part to David's character which came to the fore after he married Michelle. 'Dave looked like he was always looking over his shoulder,' said the former friend. 'He looked paranoid, I thought he was just stressed.

The reason for that stress, and David's increasing reliance on alcohol to get through his day, was easy to pinpoint – 'Crazy Shelley.'

David had met Michelle in nearby Long Beach, in North Pacific County, WA, in the mid-eighties. She already had two children – both young daughters – from an earlier marriage, but now she was divorced, and David seemed a good catch. From his point of view, his personal life was in turmoil. 'He was on the rebound' (having been dumped by another woman), said his mother, Shirley Knotek. 'He was sad and Michelle was friendly, you know how it goes.' They married and moved to Old Willapa – as rustic and wonderful as it sounds – for a number of years. Later, they would have a daughter of their own.

Before then, in 1990, their dream house came onto the market. Soon six dogs, cats, rabbits and a bird or two shared their home with the Knoteks and the children from her first marriage. The chirpily red, two storey farm house even boasted a white picket fence. The post box was decorated with sunshine symbols and pink hearts; yellow ribbons bedecked the front gate.

The welcome extended to all who passed seemed not to be limited to just looks – the Knoteks were living their dream – why not extend it to those less fortunate than themselves? But the desire to do so, on Michelle's part at least, was not driven by altruistic wishes. Her motivations were much darker than this.

'Crazy Shelley' is a not a sobriquet lightly given. Even her stepmother recognised the woman she had become. And in David, she had the sort of person who would neither challenge her excesses of behaviour not refuse to carry out her wishes.

'It didn't matter what Shelley would lie about,' she said 'he'd stick up for her. She told everyone in the family that she had cancer, and David went right along with it. In my opinion, they both bought a one-way ticket to hell.'

More casual acquaintances are less controlled in their assessment. During the media storm that followed their convictions Michelle was described as 'schizophrenic', 'evil', 'volatile' and a 'temperamental oddball' by various inhabitants of Raymond.

Small communities can be tough places for outsiders. Even more so when the population grows during the holiday season and locals have to compete with tourists on their streets. Nevertheless, with a husband as respected as David it would seem likely that Michelle would soon be accepted by the local community. That was not the case.

While not everybody was concerned by the newcomer's behaviour, even those who were less worried expressed uncertainties. Carl Carlzen was a near neighbour. He said of Michelle that the family seemed friendly and normal, even if Michelle was a little 'restless and highly strung.'

Another witness was a friend of the Knotek's daughter. She stayed over regularly, once for a whole month. This friend never witnessed the mood swings or rages that were said to typify Michelle's personality but she did note that her friend became increasingly anxious as the time for her to depart got closer.

That anxiety was for good reason, because their mother was abusive towards all three girls. Perhaps this was the main motivation for David to hang around in an increasingly difficult relationship. A friend later said, 'He stayed because of the girls. He's a loyal man.'

So there appeared to be two sides to Michelle Knotek; on the one hand an irrational woman with a violent temper who was quite prepared and able to manipulate circumstances to her own ends. On the other, a kind hearted woman with a sweet home who opened her doors to those who had fallen on tough circumstances. While such a split personality might be cause for alarm, that the second half was merely a front was even more problematic for those unfortunates who crossed her path.

Kathy Lerono Thomas was one such young lady. She had been born and grew up in Simi Valley, California but tragedy hit the family when she was just 19. Her step father was involved in a car crash and died from his injuries.

It seemed as though the Kathy was destined to face sadness in her life. Her stepfather's death followed an earlier incident when her real father was killed in a freak accident. He worked in the film industry, and was on set involved in filming a show when he was killed. The double disaster was too much for her mother, and she returned to her own family in South Bend, just down the road from Raymond.

But relationships between mothers and their teenage daughters can often be strained well into the younger person's twenties. Despite this, by nature Kathy was a positive, easy going girl determined to make the most out of a life that kept hitting major stumbling blocks. She found a job as a hairdresser and tried to settle to her new home, shared with siblings and mother but also her grandmother. Although she was welcomed, South Bend is a tight community and it can take many years for people to feel comfortable in an environment where everybody knows everybody.

Her brother Jeff found a job working down town, but Kathy was finding it much harder to discover herself. Then, when she met a boyfriend of whom her mother did not approve, matters reached a head and she decided she needed a break from the claustrophobic home to which they had travelled. Firstly, she moved in with a friend, Carolyn Barnum, who played on the same sports team as her; Kathy also baby sat Carolyn's own children. This solution was as ideal as could be given the circumstances.

But living in such a close community, it was perhaps inevitable that Kathy should come across Michelle. David was away on work (something that happened with increased frequency over time) when the two met. It is a more than reasonable supposition to think that the older woman was on the look out for somebody vulnerable and impressionable.

The relationship between the two strengthened, and Carolyn noticed a change in her friend. 'The closer she became friends with Michelle, the further she drifted away from her other friends,' the mother noted.

Then, in 1994, Carolyn was helping Kathy to find a job. They were looking for advertisements in the local shopping mall when they bumped into Michelle. She followed Kathy into the rest rooms, and Carolyn had the impression that the two were arguing. But whatever happened over the next thirty minutes, Michelle seems to have cast a spell on the young woman. When she came out of the rest rooms, she spoke briefly to the friend who had taken her in: 'I'm going to go home with Michelle,' she said. Carolyn was shocked, and recalls little of the rest of the brief exchange, other than a sense that Kathy thought she might bring trouble on her.

Whatever, it was the last time the two met. In fact, it seems as though the deal may have been sealed by a promise of accommodation in return for child care. Michelle was pregnant, and whatever arrangement was agreed upon seemed to work. In the beginning at least. But after just a few months the abuse began. It is hard for anybody to understand quite what was the motivation behind the treatment the Knotek's dished out. Suffice to say that by the end of 1991, the year in which she moved in with the couple, she had lost no less than 100 pounds in weight.

Details of the mistreatment (and there is an understated word) emerged at the Knotek's trial. Over the space of her time inside the beautiful, if childishly twee, farmhouse Kathy Loreno was forced into ever increasingly bizarre and humiliating actions. There were physical beatings and starvation. Kathy was dragged around by her hair by Michelle; and she was forced to eat rotting food and swallow random medication.

As matters escalated, she was poisoned, then forced to live and work outside – naked. The Washington State winters can be seriously cold and wet. She was made to lay down in freezing water and mud, and if she objected to this form of punishment, the Knoteks dragged her into the painful and dangerous treatment using physical force.

On occasions, further torture was inflicted – Kathy was subjected to waterboarding, a savage punishment which induces a sense of drowning and all the associated physical, mental and emotional pain.

Such was the extent of the suffering to which she was subjected that, by the time her death was close, Kathy's hair had fallen out, her teeth were gone – the few that remained were rotten and painful. Even her ability to walk or talk was lost.

When the truth finally started to come out, many years later, David claimed that he had discovered Kathy collapsed, and covered in vomit. He had tried to bring her back to life using CPR, but had failed. He claimed to police that he had not taken her to hospital, or reported her death, because injuries to her body might be seen as suspicious! By now it was 1994 and Kathy had suffered from more than two years of the most atrocious abuse imaginable. The Knoteks set fire to her body, and scattered the remains around their lot.

Inevitably, her family had become increasingly suspicious over Kathy's deterioration and then disappearance. But the story they were given varied from time to time. The consistent part was that she had simply moved out of the lodgings. Sometimes the Knoteks claimed that they did not know to where she had gone; at others she had left for Hawaii – a strange call given that even though her upbringing had been marked by tragedy, and she had fallen out with her mother, she always remained close to her brothers, Jeff and Eric Thomas. Another story spread around was that she had run off with a truck driver.

But her family were not convinced by the lies given to them. They knew what had befallen their sister and daughter. Eric said, 'We've had closure since '95. We've all known she was dead.'

The family began their own investigations; Jeff hired a private detective who concluded that his sister had been killed, but could find no witnesses to come forward. Then, in what might be seen as a decisive turn, Michelle Knotek's own step cousin, Richard Huffman, handed over to the police statements that would need to be investigated. These claimed that an un-named witness had seen Michelle Knotek torture and ultimately kill a woman, hitting her with an iron. The witness had told Michelle's step mother, Leanne Watson, of this, and via Richard the information was passed to Pacific County Deputy Sherriff, Jim Bergstrom.

'This witness saw the incident and clearly saw details surrounding the incident,' Richard said. 'That's what my aunt offered the police, very, very specific telling detail.'

The matter rested with the authorities. And rested. And rested. Over the next nine months Leanne Watson contacted the police for information repeatedly. But got no response.

Later, the Pacific County Sherriff at the time, John Didion, confirmed that the police had held information regarding Kathy's disappearance for some time. However, an administrative error had led to her case slipping down the list of priorities. Apparently, when details came in she was listed as 'an attempt to locate' situation, rather than a 'missing person'. It would prove to be a mistake with both tragic and deadly consequences.

In admitting the department's error after Michelle's ultimate arrest, Didion stated: 'We haven't had enough information to take the action that we did at the end of last week.'

Even when investigations were properly under way it seems as though communication from the Pacific County police department were lacking in consistency. One deputy claimed with some accuracy that Kathy had been murdered by Michelle Knotek and then buried in their yard; Jeff Loreno said that the detective in receipt of the original witness claims, Jim Bergstrom, told him that Kathy had been struck and killed with an iron, then burned. However, he would not enlarge on the evidence for his theory. However, Bergstrom's claim was made more than eight months before the Knotek's subsequent arrest.

Errors occur; that is a part of life. Unfortunately, by the time the police realised their mistake at least one, possibly two and maybe more murders had also been committed. But before then, a killing even closer to home would take place.

Shane Watson was a sweet natured young man. He enjoyed being outdoors, taking part in wholesome activities – the opposite to popular views of teenage boys. Sadly for him, he was also Michelle Knotek's nephew. One of his favourite activities was to chop wood with David.

In fact, such was the bond with his uncle that when he entered his late teens, in the early 1990s, Shane took the decision to move out of his grandparent's home, and in with David and Michelle. Unfortunately, his early life in Tacoma, Washington, had been troubled and following a highly acrimonious divorce between his parents, he had moved in with his grandparents. But by the early 1990s, his grandfather's health had taken a turn for the worse, and to move into his Aunt and Uncle's spacious farmhouse seemed a sensible decision. All parties expressed their happiness with the arrangements.

'He had finally the friend he had always wanted,' said his grandmother.

But despite his fondness for his uncle, Shane was a young man with a sense of moral propriety. He observed the ongoing and increasing mistreatment of Kathy Loreno and began to keep a record of what was going on, including taking a photograph of the abuse.

Michelle discovered it, and began to beat her family guest. What caused the events of just two weeks later is hard to determine because there was only one witness, and his story lacked consistency.

Yet what is not denied is that Shane Watson was shot and killed. David's first story was that he had come across Shane with a .22 calibre rifle, something from which he had been banned from using. An argument ensued which came to physical as well as verbal blows. During this exchange, David had attempted to take the gun away from his nephew, and it had inadvertently discharged, killing the younger man.

But David's story was soon to change. Under questioning, he said that he had shot Shane in the back – something he hugely regretted. However, he told the police that he feared that his nephew would 'go into a bar and spill all the information about Kathy Loreno.'

David was left with a body, a murder weapon and a lot of mess. He used bleach to clear up the blood, then burned the remains of Shane. He tried to do the same with the gun but only the wooden stock would succumb – he stored the remainder, including the barrel, in the laundry room.

When his grandparents called, Shane had 'just gone out,'; at other times he had moved in with a girlfriend, or gone fishing in Alaska.

Kathy Loreno and Shane Watson were not the last of the Knotek's victims. Ronald Wordworth, known as Woody, was another vulnerable person. In middle age he moved to Raymond from California with the intention of taking care of his elderly mother. But his partner could not cope with the change, and left. It seems as though Woody endured a difficult, life changing time. He had been an active member of the Lions Club, a volunteer worker and a successful proof reader with the local newspaper, the Willapa Harbor Herald, where he was well liked and highly regarded by his colleagues.

Then, it all went wrong. The man blessed with the rare and dying skill of being a hieroglyphics reader started to get into trouble with the law. He was charged for check fraud; he had anti-harassment orders cast against him. He seemed to lose his mind. A neighbour reported that Woody developed the strange habit of hiding in ditches, and jumping out at passers-by.

Matters deteriorated to such an extent that soon Woody was looking for somewhere to live. Michelle Knotek gladly obliged. And in 2001 Ronald Wordworth moved in with the couple about whom the police were sitting on information. The abuse started almost immediately. Firstly, it was minor physical attacks from Michelle; Woody was a small man, just 5' 6" tall, and Michelle a very aggressive woman.

Soon the abuse escalated and David became involved, punching his victim in the mouth if he showed any dissent towards the behaviour he was made to endure. Matters got ever worse – he was made to work in the cold yard, wearing only a bathrobe and a hat; he was forced to jump barefoot onto rough gravel; at one point, his feet were doused in boiling water until the skin peeled from his flesh.

The last sighting of Woody was on July 20th 2003; whether he just died, or an attack from Michelle went too far is uncertain. The claims of the couple were that their lodger committed suicide. Apparently, on the 22nd of the same month, David received a call from work to say that Woody had killed himself. He came home and buried the victim in his garden.

Of course, the question comes to mind as to why these three victims – as well as their own children – put up with the abuse the Knotek's inflicted? There are many possible reasons. All were vulnerable people – in the children's case, that vulnerability caused by their own parents. Each of the three who died was at least partially estranged from their family. They were alone, or close to it, in the world. Then, they became trapped in the Knotek's environment. Wives and partners in violent relationships often find it hard to get away from their abusive spouses. In addition, nobody finds it easy to consider themselves a victim, and it is human nature to believe that things are not as bad as they seem. Sadly, sometimes they are.

There was also a more practical reason making it hard for the victims to get away. Simply, the Knoteks installed heavy duty locks on their rooms. They were not prepared to take any risks.

The death of Woody was enough to get neighbours and witnesses to open their mouths. Firstly, the Knotek's daughter, herself the victim of abuse, spoke, and soon the public were offering more details.

Michelle claimed on her arrest that (like her other victims) Woody had simply gone away. She said that David had driven him to nearby Olympia, and from there he had caught a bus south to San Diego.

When it came to trial in 2004, Michelle faced charges of first degree murder for the deaths of Woody Woodworth and Kathy Loreno. David stood to be convicted for the murder of Shane, and a number of offences related to the other deaths. Plea mitigation took place, with Michelle coming to rely on an Alford plea. Named after a 1970 case in which Henry Alford pleaded guilty to second degree murder to avoid the death penalty, this means that, while not admitting guilt of the crimes for which a person is charged, they accept that the evidence against them means that they are likely to be convicted.

Michelle received a twenty two year prison sentence, David fifteen years – he is eligible for parole in 2019.

It did not end there. By the 2000s Michelle was working in the care industry. It was while she was supporting 81 year old James McClintock – Mac – that he 'fell', striking his head and dying as medical and police support arrived. He left his estate to his Labrador, Sissy, with a healthy sum set aside for Michelle to look after the animal. When it too died just six months later, Michelle inherited the entire estate. In fact, Woody Woodworth was working on the house to get it ready for resale when he too died.

The circumstances around McClintock's death were sufficiently unclear for Michelle to be considered a strong suspect in his case, although there has never been enough evidence to charge her. People who work with the elderly must become used to death, but a taste of suspicion surrounds every patient who died under Michelle Knotek's watch. A woman once described as being 'indifferent to human life', she fits into a small but particularly unpleasant category of those convicted of murder.

There are people wrongly imprisoned; those who kill in passion, or for their own personal gain such as when committing a robbery. There are even those who kill to send a message to others, when under the influence of drugs or alcohol and there are those who claim that the loss of others' lives is an acceptable price to pay for getting across a political point. Michelle Knotek does not fit into these categories. It seems as though she killed simply because she could. Because she was unconcerned by the suffering she caused. All killing is evil but there are many who consider a murderer such as Michelle Knotek as being of the very worst kind.

HUSBAND KILLER : THE TRUE STORY OF MARY WINKLER

JAMES FALCON

The Case of Mary Winkler

Mary Winkler, at first appearances, would seem to be an altogether normal woman. So too did her family, with a husband who was a Church minister and three young children, girls aged just eight, six and one.

The family lived in Selmer, Tenn., a small town occupied by around 4,500 people, according to the 2015 census. The town is situated to the south west of the state. Not much has happened in Selmer; the most famous person to have been born there was Chad Harville, former pitcher for the Oakland A's, and for one year, the Red Sox. He achieved a 4-9 win-loss record over his career in the MLB.

Today, the most famous- or infamous- person to have come from Selmer is Mary Winkler. In 2006, Mary sparked a border-crossing manhunt, and a court case followed nationwide. She had killed her husband with a shot to the back from the family's shotgun. But it was the gripping, and at times bizarre, court case which gripped the attention of the nation.

Matthew dead, Mary and the family Missing

The date was March 6th, 2007. It was a Tuesday like any other. Mary and Matthew were at home all day together, although Matthew was due to give a sermon that evening.

It was actually members of Matthew's congregation who found his body that night. They had visited his home to check up on him after he had missed the service he was set to give; instead, they found him lying dead, having been shot in the back.

There was no sign of Mary or any of their children at the home, and as such, they were reported missing. The authorities quickly sent out an Amber Alert, since nobody had any idea what could have happened to them, or where they might be. Family and friends had no information to provide police on their whereabouts.

There was every chance that the family had been kidnapped or murdered, and their bodies disposed of elsewhere, although police could not identify a break in, and had no reason to believe that anything of value had been stolen.

It was only a day later that she was arrested in Alabama, having run from the family home with her young children. They were found 350 miles away from home, at Orange Beach, and in the back seat of the van was the family's shotgun. It was certainly suspicious; but what reason could Mary have possibly had for committing such a crime?

The Trial

In the build up to the case going to trial, public interest ramped up. Speculation had been rife about why Mary would have murdered her husband, a seemingly nice, well respected member of the local community. Perhaps either one of them had had an affair, and Matthew had been killed in a crime of passion. Or maybe he had been killed for an insurance claim?

As such, the press reported every step of the story as it came out during the hearing. The trial began when a Tennessee Bureau of Investigation Agent John Mehr read a statement that Mary had made very soon after her arrest. In it, Mary claimed that the couple had been arguing about their family finances, before Mary had shot her husband with their 12 gauge shotgun. She had said that the last thing she had wanted was to actually murder her husband, but she had been brandishing the gun in an effort to convince him to work through their problems, together. The argument had been ongoing throughout the day, and Mary had finally snapped, resorting to drastic measures to be able to convince him. She had never intended to kill him: she had said in the statement, 'I don't want this at all. I don't want any of this to be, at all.'

The statement continued on, and Mary claimed that they had argued often and argued fiercely. 'He had really been on me lately,' Mary had said, 'criticizing me for things- the way I walk, I eat, everything. It was just building up to a point. I was tired of it. I guess I got to a point and snapped.'

At first glance, it would seem that Mary had simply lost her composure, become angry, and killed her husband 'as the red mist had descended'. But after their initial statement, Mary's attorney indicated that there was much more that would come out about Matthew's behaviour when she testified which would help to explain her actions. Clearly, there were more problems with their marriage than the occasional, albeit fierce, argument.

Mary's Crime

The case for the prosecution wasted no time in painting Mary as a cold blooded killer, who left her husband to die without remorse. Admittedly, the plain facts of the case made Mary seem unbelievably guilty. The prosecution relied on several of these facts in their attempt to convince the jury of Mary's guilt for the charge of murder.

Mary had disconnected the phone immediately after she shot her husband, stopping him from being able to call the emergency services, or receive any calls that may have come in. This suggested that Mary had been in full control of her actions, not panicking, since it is unlikely that somebody in a state of anxiety would think to disconnect the phone.

The fact that Mary had attempted to flee to Orange Beach, Alabama, was also a key point for the prosecution. Immediately after Matthew's death, Mary had taken the family minivan to the beach, with her three children. Later on in her defence, Mary would claim that she ran because '[n]obody would believe me, and they'd take the girls away and put me away.' Certainly, in many murder cases, the fact that the defendant flees the scene is a certain indicator of guilt.

The family's daughter Patricia testified that she couldn't understand her mother's actions. All that she knew was that she had heard a 'big boom', and the sound of something heavy hitting the floor. She quickly ran to the bedroom to see her father on the floor, and her mother holding the shotgun. She had no idea what could possibly have provoked her mother to shoot him.

Another sticking point was that the family finances had been 'in shambles' just before the murder had taken place. This had led Mary to become embroiled in what is called a 'check kiting' scam. In it, she had received checks from unidentified accounts in Canada and Nigeria, and had ultimately fallen to a financial scam that had lost the family money. Prosecutors claimed that this could have somehow instigated the argument that led to Matthew's death, and that Mary had felt as if she had no way out of the scam.

They also jumped on the fact that in an initial conversation with investigators, Mary had told them that their marriage was a happy one, and that '[t]here's no poor me. I'm in control.' They clearly wanted to paint a picture of Mary as remorseless, deceitful, and smarter than she looked.

The Cross-examination

During her cross-examination in court, Mary stated that she didn't remember grabbing the gun from the closet in which it was kept. What she did remember was that 'something went off', 'hearing a loud boom', and that 'it wasn't as loud as I thought it would be.' She did admit that she had shot her husband. Matthew rolled from the bed- upon which he had been lying as they had argued- and dropped to the floor. Mary described smelling gunpowder.

Prosecutor Walter Freeland asked her whether she understood that 'pulling a trigger is what makes it go boom', to which she replied that she did.

Matthew asked her why she had snapped and shot him. She could only say 'I'm sorry.' The shotgun blast had been inflicted from behind, directly into Matthew's back, and had caused severe damage to his organs and spine. According to prosecutors, he had in fact still been alive as Mary had run from the house.

But these simple facts were far from the end of the story, as Mary was to reveal.

Appearances and Revelations

At first, Mary spoke of her husband not in the past tense, but in the present, as if she couldn't quite understand how final her actions really had been. In reminiscing about happier times, Mary told the court that her husband was an intelligent, social man, and that the family had shared many 'good times' together. She also seemed to enjoy talking about her children, and the happiness they brought her.

This happy family life, however, was simply one side of the marriage. Mary's attorney stated that '[w]hat went on behind their closed doors is going to have to be told ... Some of what we've got from the state of Tennessee touches on sexual abuse.' Their defence was that Matthew had made Mary's life a 'living hell': '[w]e will show you proof that he would destroy objects that she loved, he would isolate her from her family and he would abuse her not just verbally, not just emotional and not just physically—in other ways, too.'

Just before the murder, Mary claimed that Matthew had been threatening their children and even attempted to throttle their infant daughter, Breanna. He had been shouting, angry, because he had wanted a son. As the case went on, it became obvious that this was only the tip of the iceberg, however, and more and more sordid details of their home life would come to light.

Matthew, Mary claimed, was a violent, abusive husband. Shortly after their marriage, he ordered her to stop socialising with any of her family and friends (a common tactic among abusive spouses in order to further isolate their partners from potential help). Winkler's sisters described how Mary seemed stuck in her marriage, unhappy, but unable to leave. In an interview, they said that 'As the years went on, she seemed to be nervous to show love towards us.'

Mary was commonly 'screamed and hollered' at by her husband. 'He just flailed. He's a big guy and he was just all over ... He'd point his finger inches away from my nose. Whatever he was upset about, it was my fault,' Mary had said. It could be over anything: 'I was fat, my hair wasn't right, the girls, if something went wrong, it was my fault. I didn't know when it was coming.' Mary described her situation as one familiar to abused wives and husbands across America.

Her attorney, Steve Farese, provided further information based on his conversations with Mary. She had needed her husband's permission for everything, even for getting her hair cut. 'This was constant, and she lived a life where she walked on eggshells.' This abuse, he said, had given Mary symptoms of post traumatic stress disorder, simply because 'she didn't know what was going to happen next.' Furthermore, a psychologist testified as part of Mary's defence, saying that her symptoms were those of clinical depression and PTSD.

During her time on the stand, Mary also claimed that Matthew had forced her to watch pornography with him, and that he had bought her several 'slutty' costumes for sex, which she normally would never have worn, but for fear of her husband. If she refused, Matthew wouldn't hesitate to get physical, hitting her or even using his belt to whip her. Mary famously produced a wig and a pair of white high heels in the witness box during her cross-examination to show the court evidence of Matthew's other side.

Mary stated that she was never happy watching pornography, dressing up in sexy outfits or performing the sex acts that Matthew wanted. She went along with his ideas, however, because she didn't dare face his reaction if she didn't. 'I'd just do anything to help him stay happy.' Throughout these revelations, Mary was visibly embarrassed and uncomfortable. Clearly she would have preferred that none of them had ever come to light; but Mary felt it necessary to brave what her neighbors, and the nation, might think in order to clear her name and justify her actions.

Mary's family had been quick to corroborate her side of the story. Her father, Clark Freeman, had spoken out through Good Morning America and detailed the 'physical, mental, verbal' abuse that his daughter had suffered. Other friends came forward during the court case, and gave similar verdicts on their relationship. A friend of Mary's, Rudie Thomsen, said that '[o]ne Sunday, Mary came into the church and I looked at her and she had a black eye.' Similarly, Mary's friend Amy Redmon agreed that Matthew had been controlling: '[h]e was an authority figure, and he made the decisions basically. It was obvious.'

Conversely, Matthew's family denied that their son had been anything like Mary had depicted in her defence testimony. Matthew's father, Charles Daniel Winkler, said that his son was a kind, gentle man, who could have done nothing to justify what the defence was claiming. Diane spoke several times during the trial, lashing out at Mary: 'You've never told your girls you're sorry! Don't you think you at least owe them that?'

The dramatic story of a supposedly kindly, gentle church minister having such a sordid, cruel and abusive hidden life gripped America. The case was covered extensively on all major networks, discussed on late night panel shows

The Jury's Verdict

While the prosecutors had tried to convince the jury to convict her on a charge of first degree murder, they were unsuccessful. The jury came to their verdict by April, that year. It took them eight hours to deliberate their way to the decision; this mirrored the response of the nation, which was similarly undecided on just what punishment Mary really deserved.

Mary was found guilty of voluntary manslaughter, a charge which carries a far more lenient sentence than murder. While murderers can receive full life sentences, and in certain states receive the death penalty, the maximum sentence for voluntary manslaughter is only 6 years.

Mary showed little emotion at the verdict, but did embrace each of her relatives afterwards. In a show of support, her family had been sat in the row behind her, and all linked arms with one another to demonstrate their solidarity. Afterwards, she was taken back into custody to await sentencing.

Mary's attorney stated afterwards that Mary's testimony had been central in securing the more lenient sentence. 'I think Mary's testimony was integral in this decision. They had to hear it from Mary', Farese told the press. 'They judged her credibility and they saw that she had an abusive relationship and they made their judgment based upon that.'

For Mary, the most important implication of the verdict was that she could finally begin to think of being reunited with her children. Speaking on her behalf after the trial, Farese continued: 'We would like to do so many things to open up communication between Mary and the paternal grandparents and to get the children out of this cycle of constant upheaval over this terrible tragic event.' But the question of how long she would be in prison remained.

Mary's sentencing was scheduled for May 18th, at which point both Mary and the prosecution would have a final chance to address the court before the judge decided on the final jail term. However, the situation looked positive for Mary. Not only would the five months that she had been imprisoned awaiting trial be taken into consideration, but the judge had indicated that alternatives to incarceration would be on the table. Perhaps Mary could avoid jail time altogether.

Sentencing: The Trial at an End

Due to a scheduling error, the hearing took place around three weeks late, on June 8th.

Mary took to the stand one last time to plead for mercy. She read aloud from a prepared statement, telling Matthew's family of her sorrow and remorse for her actions. She was 'so sorry that this had happened', and would 'always miss and love' her husband. 'I ask for mercy and understanding, but I know whatever decision you reach today will be right ... I ask you to please let me go home today and be with my children.' Tabitha Freeman- Mary's sister- had also pleaded for leniency, in particular to let Mary be reunited with her children. She went as far as calling Mary 'the best example of a good person I can think of'.

Members of Matthew's family, too, took to the stand to plead their case for the prosecution. Charles and his wife were clearly hurt and in disbelief at Mary's actions both in murdering their son, and believed that Mary had purposefully smeared his name at trial. 'The monster that you have painted for the world to see? I don't think that monster existed,' Diane Winkler had said.

After speaking their pieces, all that Mary, her family, and Matthew's parents could do was wait until the judge's decision. The trial- as well as the very public 'trial' that Mary had been through in the media- was finally at an end.

The defence had requested that Mary be granted full probation, or judicial diversion, both outcomes which would have meant that Mary would spent no further time in prison, and even that her record would be cleared of wrongdoing altogether. This request was denied.

After recess, Mary was told that she would spend 3 years in prison for her crime. But Circuit Judge J. Weber McCraw reduced that amount to just 210 days total in prison before she would be allowed to leave on probation. She also had that sentence reduced further, due to the fact that she had spent five months incarcerated waiting for trial.

Moreover, that time would be spent not in jail, but in a mental health centre in Tennessee. There, she would receive treatment for both her depression and post traumatic stress disorder. After such a long ordeal, with the prosecution fighting to either put Mary on death row or to imprison her indefinitely, it seemed that she had gotten off with hardly a slap on the wrist.

Steve Farese branded the sentence 'a victory': '[s]he could be in prison for life, and that's what everybody thought she was headed for to begin with.' Her other attorney, Leslie Ballin, said '[s]he'll be able to get out and fight the battle she wants to, and that is to get her children back.' Mary could finally think about the future again.

But certain signs indicated that it would not be as easy to reconcile with her children and family as she might hope. Matthew's family left the courtroom without making a comment to the press, as did the prosecution, clearly disappointed in the verdict. They gave no indication that they would be happy to open dialogue about Mary's daughters- not with the woman whom they believed to have murdered their son in cold blood.

The aftermath of Mary's release

Mary was released on August 14th, 2007. She had only been sentenced the previous June.

Upon her release, her lawyer informed the press that Mary would not be speaking with them, to maintain her privacy. During her time in the mental health facility, Mary could finally begin her attempt to win full custody of her three daughters, and she was still fighting this case at the time of her release. She had not seen her children, apart from Patricia's brief testimony as part of the case, for over a year. Throughout the case, and after Mary's release, her children were staying with Matthew's family.

Moreover, she was still fighting a $2 million dollar civil lawsuit filed by Matthew's parents. They also took legal measures, which, if successful, would have meant that the custody of Mary's children remained with them.

After her release, Mary seemed happier to her family and friends. From an outside perspective, it could be easy to claim that this was just as much due to her happiness at avoiding a jail sentence as it was to her being rid of an abuser. She was in fact living with friends at first after her release, and went back to work at a dry cleaners in McMinnville, Tenn., 200 miles from Selmer.

In the same interview as was mentioned before, Mary's sisters agreed that she had changed entirely. After years of shyness, Mary seeming unable or unwilling to show love to them for fear of her husband's violence, she seemed to finally be able to open up. 'Now it's back to the old Mary [who] loves us and doesn't care to come and hug us and gives us a kiss on the cheek.'

Since then, Mary lived in McMinnville. She has moved between jobs, working at the dry cleaners, before starting work at a nursery. She briefly dated the brother of one of her most vocal supporters, Paul Pillow; afterwards, she moved in with Wayne Cantrell, a preacher living in Smithville nearby.

Mary regained custody of her three children in 2008, but by 2010, received the news that she had multiple sclerosis. Her diagnosis came at the worst time, as she was settling down in her new life; she had not long started medical school with the desire to become a nurse, and had to quit since the work would be too demanding. She hasn't returned to work since.

One comfort for Mary was that Matthew's parents seemed close to being able to forgive her. After her diagnosis, they gave Mary some time off from parenting by taking care of the children for a weekend, which soon turned into several months. Daniel Winkler has preached several times since the events on the topic of forgiveness, although when asked by local press why he chose the topic, he has refused to answer, presumably preferring to keep those details private.

Mary, too, preferred to put the past behind her. In an interview with WAFF 48, the NBC affiliate in Huntsville AL., she stated how she would prefer to stay out of the limelight, particularly for the sake of her girls. 'Whatever reason people have any problem with me, that's fine. Everybody's entitled to their opinion, but these girls are treated for who they are, not because of what their mother's done ... They're three very fine young ladies'.

Concluding Thoughts

Some members of the public reacted with disgust at the abnormally short sentence that Mary was given, and questioned whether a husband would have been given the same leniency as Mary was. Men's rights activist Glenn Sacks publicly questioned whether a man would have been shown such leniency, and pointed to the case of Scott Peterson (who received the death penalty for the murder of his pregnant wife) to indicate that no, a man would not. He also argued that the idea of abuse had been widened to include simple criticism, and should therefore not necessarily be used as defence of murder.

Conversely, there have been many women put in prison for murdering their abusive husbands, some for much longer than Mary Winkler. The 'battered woman defense', or the preferred terminology today of 'battering and its effects', is not a genuine legal defence in itself; it can, however, be used to convince a court of diminished responsibility. Its effectiveness is due to the sympathy that it elicits from jurors, who can be convinced that abuse is a form of provocation, and the murder a form of self defense. Under this defense, Mary's short sentence makes sense.

The case has remained a touch stone with regards to spousal abuse in the U.S. A made-for-TV movie, 'The Pastor's Wife', was released in 2011. It was based on the book of the same title, written by Dianne Fanning, an award winning crime writer. The story was changed somewhat, with the inclusion of a financial subplot involving tax fraud. However, it also made use of real life interviews with people who knew the Winklers- including Matthew's parents. His mother revealed that she could never believe Mary's story. Charles admitted that Mary's story could be true, and that he could forgive her if she confessed her purposeful intention to murder Matthew.

As for the community in which the family had lived, the reaction was largely one of forgiveness. According to members of that community, the town's 'Christian roots and ... its tendency to give people the benefit of the doubt' meant that they took Mary at her word. Mary's quite life in McMinnville and Smithville similarly shows that the American public would rather leave her and her family alone after their painful ordeal.

The Crimes of The Papin Sisters

Amy Delaney

The Papin Sisters

Clémence Derré did not have the best reputation. She was well known for being promiscuous and was not a desirable candidate for Gustave Papin, whose parents disliked the girl, especially after finding out about her affair with her boss. She was the talk of the town, but Gustave was in love, and nothing anybody else could say or do would change his mind. Besides which, Clémence was pregnant with Gustave's baby, and Gustave wanted to do the right thing.

On October 3rd, 1901, Gustave Papin and Clémence Derré were married, and four months later on February 12th, 1902, their daughter Emilia was born.

However, things did not go the way Gustave had imagined. His young wife had absolutely no interest in either her new daughter, or in fact, her husband, and showed little affection to either.

Gustave's suspicions began to grow. Having steadfastly stood by Clémence when the town people had turned against her, he now began to believe that maybe the rumours had been true after all. He started to wonder if it was possible that his wife had not only had an affair with her boss but was still doing so.

Gustave made several attempts to catch his wife out – lying in wait whenever and wherever he thought they might be, but his efforts proved futile.

With his jealousy growing, Gustave decided that the only solution would be to move his wife and daughter away from the town altogether, taking Clémence out of temptation's way.

Gustave set about turning his plans into reality, and in July 1904 he secured himself a position at a saw mill in Marigné, 8km away, believing it to be a second chance for the couple. However, Clémence was furious – she had no desire to leave her home or her lover and reacted by threatening suicide. But by this time she was pregnant with the couple's second child, so she resigned herself to starting a new life in a new village, knowing that nobody else would want a pregnant woman.

On March 8th, 1905, their second child was born – another little girl whom they named Christine. But if Gustave was hoping for a reversal of the state of their marriage he was disappointed, as the relationship disintegrated even further.

Married life was not how Gustave imagined it to be – his wife complained bitterly about her constant tiredness and her unwillingness to look after their daughters, so Gustave took matters into his own hands, and sent Christine to live with his elder sister Isabelle, who also lived in Marigné.

In August 1910 Gustave and Clémence settled in Le Mans with their daughter Emilia, and on September 15th, 1911 Clémence gave birth again, to a third daughter whom they named Léa.[1]

Christine

Christine was happy at her Aunt Isabelle's. Isabelle had a deep mistrust of men but had always wanted to be a mother, so when she was given the opportunity to take in a baby to raise as her own, she jumped at the chance. Isabelle's own mother had been destroyed, at least in Isabelle's eyes, by numerous pregnancies, and she was adamant she was not going to go the same way. She had worked as a maid and when her elderly employer died, Isabelle was left a small inheritance. She was fiercely independent and greatly disapproved of Christine's mother for her various involvements with men. According to Isabelle, as long as a woman stayed away from men she would be safe.

But Christine absorbed her Aunt's hatred of men, and in turn developed her own distrust of them.

Rape

Sometime around Léa's birth, a shocking secret emerged. Clémence found out that her husband, Gustave, had raped their first born daughter, Emilia, who would have been only around ten at the time. Clémence reacted with fury, but she not only directed that fury at her husband but also at her daughter Emilia, whom Clémence believed had seduced Gustave. There was talk of Emilia not being Gustave's daughter, and Clémence assumed that the little girl had been a willing sexual partner to her father, and had enjoyed it.

Clémence took her revenge on both of them.

She divorced Gustave, as one would expect for such a heinous crime, but she also took revenge on Emilia, sending her away to a religious orphanage called Le Bon Pasteur. The orphanage had a reputation for harshness, and Clémence thought it might force her 'errant' daughter to mend her ways. At the same time, Clémence removed Christine from Isabelle's care and placed her alongside her sister at the orphanage. Baby Léa was given to a great-uncle to be looked after, and Clémence, now both husband and child free, obtained work as a maid.[2]

Léa

Léa stayed with her uncle until 1918, when she was around seven. When her uncle died, Clémence placed Léa into a religious institution in Le Mans[3], where she would stay until 1924.

Emilia

Not a lot is known about Emilia Papin, except that, after her time at Le Bon Pasteur, she decided to enter the convent and dedicate her life to the church. As far as records show, she spent the rest of her life there.[4]

Back to Christine

Christine was set to follow in her older sister's footsteps – she, too, wanted to join a convent. While she had had Emilia at Le Bon Pasteur with her, she had felt protected and loved, but with Emilia now in a convent, Christine found herself alone. The love she had felt for Emilia now had nowhere to go, as entering the convent no doubt meant excommunicating herself from her family. So Christine turned her affections towards her little sister, Léa.

Christine's plans were scuppered by Clémence, however. The woman had been furious when Emilia had joined the convent, as she had been getting to an age when she could go out to work and earn money to send to her mother. So when Christine decided she wanted the same life, Clémence put her foot down, exercising her parental rights.[5]

At that time, in France, the age of majority was 21, meaning that parents had the deciding say on what their children did up until that time. So Clémence, seeing her meal ticket disappearing the same way it had with Emilia, prevented Christine from joining a convent and instead committed her to a life of service.

Christine was well suited to the life of a maid – she had spent eight years at Le Bon Pasteur where she had been expertly taught in skills such as housekeeping and sewing.

Christine found work easily enough, but she was forced to leave several jobs because, according to her mother, the pay wasn't enough for her (Clémence's) needs.

When Léa was old enough, she too went into service, and the two sisters often worked together in the various homes of their employers.

The Lancelins

In 1926, when Christine was 22, she managed to secure a position with the Lancelin family in Le Mans.

René Lancelin was a retired lawyer, who lived at No. 6 rue Bruyère, with his wife, Léonie, and their grown-up daughter, Geneviève. The couple had another daughter who lived away from home.

When Christine had been working for the Lancelins for two months, she asked them if they would consider hiring Léa as well. Madame Lancelin was impressed with the standard of Christine's work, so she agreed to take on her younger sister too.

Life went on, with Christine working as the cook and Léa as the chambermaid. The girls were diligent with their work, putting in 12-14 hour days and working six and a half days a week. Their only time off was a half day on Sundays when the girls would attend church, dressed appropriately, with gloves and hats.

The sisters had no interests outside of each other and the church, apart from an occasional visit to a local medium, and the remainder of their time was spent in the attic room they shared. They showed no interest in meeting suitors, or dancing, or going to the movies.[6]

At first, it would seem that the sisters had a reasonable relationship with Madame Lancelin. When their employer found out that they were sending their wages to their mother, Clémence, she urged them to stop passing it on and keep it for themselves. She even went so far as to tell Clémence herself that her 'gravy train' had now stopped. The girls' wages were around 3000 francs per year, which amounts to around $2236 today.[7]

Because of Madame Lancelin's kindness, the sisters began referring to her as 'Maman' in private.

Although their living arrangements were basic – the sisters shared one small bed in the attic for instance – they had a balcony from which they could watch the people of Le Mans pass by. It was a relative luxury among the serving community.[8] Indeed, as servants go, the sisters had it better than most. There was always plenty to eat, and the girls had a heated bedroom, a luxury which many other servants of the time were denied.

The Tide Turns

After a few years, things began to take a downward turn in the Lancelin household. Although both the girls had an enviable reputation with regards to their work, their personalities seemed to cause some consternation among other people. Local shopkeepers found the girls to be aloof and reserved, and one woman, who herself had employed Christine for a couple of weeks, described her time with Christine as difficult, stating that she found the girl so touchy and rebellious that she was loath to ask her to do anything. Nonetheless, their professional standing was second to none – unlike other maids of the time, the sisters did not engage in any flirtations with local boys and applied themselves meticulously to their duties.

Despite Madame Lancelin's initial kindness in ensuring the girls got to keep their wages, she became an increasingly hard taskmaster and took to wearing white gloves to check that the sisters had left no dust anywhere.

Communication became stinted. Madame Lancelin would only communicate with Christine and not Léa, and even then it would invariably be via a typed message regarding their work rather than through actual conversation.

Monsieur Lancelin himself later admitted that he had never once spoken to Christine or Léa during their seven years of service in his house.[9]

Sisterly Love

The fact that the sisters spent so much time together alone in their room did not go unnoticed. Christine was also fiercely protective of Léa, and was apparently extremely jealous of Genevieve Lancelin, whenever she attempted to initiate conversation with the younger sister. On one of the girls' visits to the local medium, they had apparently been told that Christine had been Léa's husband in a past life, a belief which she seemed to act out. In fact, such was the abnormality of the closeness and affection the sisters shared for each other that Madame Lancelin and her family began to suspect that the two young women were engaged in sexual relations.[10]

The sisters were unnaturally close, described by some that knew them as obsessive. They would braid each other's hair, make clothes for each other, and spent every moment together, completely shunning any outside interests. On one occasion, Madame Lancelin took it upon herself to spy on the women and had her suspicions confirmed when she caught the sisters making love. One can only imagine the shock – at the time homosexuality was very much frowned upon, and when you add incest to the mix it became even more scandalous. To the girls, though, their behaviour probably felt completely normal. Their own father had raped their sister, and their Aunt had consistently warned against the perils of mixing with men.[11] Their father had disappeared from their lives after his sexual abuse of Emelia had come out, apparently fighting in World War One and subsequently re-marrying[12]) and they had found in each other the affection and love that their own mother had been unwilling or unable to provide. The love they had for each other was the only love they had ever truly known. Madame Lancelin decided to share what she had seen with the rest of her family, but for one reason or another no action was taken, and life carried on.

The situation became more strained after a particular incident involving Léa and Madame Lancelin. While cleaning the floor, Léa had missed a tiny scrap of paper, which Madame Lancelin noticed, and, enraged by the girl's inattention to detail, pinched Léa hard and viciously until she was forced to her knees to pick up the offending piece of paper. Léa, who was normally very quiet and withdrawn, told Christine *"She had better not try that again or I will defend myself."*[13]

Christine's Descent into Madness

Towards the end of 1932, Christine's behaviour began to change. She began to suffer explosive fits of anger which she directed at her younger sister, Léa. The previously loving, albeit unnatural, relationship became a frightening ordeal for the younger sister as she could do nothing but suffer her older sister's outbursts which came from nowhere. Her normally kind demeanour was slowly changing into that of someone totally alien to her.

The pair continued to perform their duties for the Lancelin family, but Christine was losing her grip on reality. She began to suffer from hallucinations – seeing and hearing things which were not there, and these episodes, which today would have been recognized as symptoms of paranoid schizophrenia, in turn, set off panic attacks in Léa, who could not cope with her sister's state of mind, and behaviour.

It was all about to come to a tragic and fatal head.

February 2nd, 1933

The late winter was making its presence felt in Le Mans on February 2nd, 1933. It was bitterly cold, and the wind was howling outside.[14] Madame Lancelin had spent the day shopping with her daughter, Genevieve, and the pair were due to meet Monsieur Lancelin at his brother in law's house for dinner later that evening. Christine and Léa were not expecting their employer home until late into the night.

One of Léa's jobs for that day had been to take a broken iron to the electrician's to be fixed. However, when she returned home and plugged it in ready to do some ironing, it shorted the power to the entire house. As the Lancelins weren't due home until late that night, Christine took the decision to leave fixing the fuse until the next morning.

However, Madame and Genevieve Lancelin did return home, sometime after 5.30 pm, and were annoyed to find the house in darkness. Christine met them at the door and explained that the iron had been fixed, but that when it had been plugged in it had shorted the power. Madame Lancelin was furious at this news and a row broke out.

It was enough to tip Christine over the edge.

The older sister grabbed a pewter jug and brought it down onto Madame Lancelin's head. Her daughter, Genevieve, heard the commotion and came rushing to her mother's aid, only to receive a similar blow. As Christine began to fight with Genevieve, Léa joined in, struggling with Madame Lancelin, who had managed to recover somewhat from the blow. As the fight continued in the darkness, Christine shouted: *"I'm going to massacre them."*

As the fight became more frenzied, Christine began to shout orders to her sister.

"Smash her head into the ground" and *"tear her eyes out"*!

Léa had always followed her older sister's orders, and she wasn't about to stop now. With her bare hands, she gouged Madame Lancelin's eyes out, while Christine did the same thing to Genevieve.

As the two women lay writhing, blind and in agony on the floor, the sisters went on the search for weapons with which to continue their brutal attack. Finding a knife and a hammer, they returned to the grisly scene, and systematically beat their employers with first the pewter jug, and then the hammer. Mercifully for the Lancelin women, death came at last. But, even though they could no longer feel it, their mutilation was far from over.

The Papin sisters then 'prepared' the bodies of the two women as if they were preparing a joint of meat for dinner, carving deep gashes into their flesh. Lifting the skirts of the two women over their heads, leaving them with no dignity whatsoever, the maids sliced into their thighs and buttocks. Their final act of humiliation was to smear Madame Lancelin's body with Genevieve's menstrual blood, basting her as they would baste a joint of beef.

The Discovery

While his wife and daughter were being slaughtered in their own home, Monsieur Lancelin was at first irritated, and then worried, when they failed to show up for dinner. He made the journey home to pick them up, but when he arrived he couldn't get in. The house was locked and bolted from the inside. He thought it strange that the maids hadn't answered the door, but decided that perhaps they hadn't heard him and that his wife and daughter had already left for Madame Lancelin's brother's house.

When he returned to his brother in law's house, however, there was still no sign of his wife or daughter, and Monsieur Lancelin began to worry. Enlisting the help of a dinner guest, he returned once more to his house, but he still could not get inside. Furthermore, the house was in darkness apart from a candle flickering in the window of the maids' attic bedroom.

Finally, he went to the police with his concerns.

One of the policemen who returned to the house with Monsieur Lancelin climbed the wall at the back of the house and gained entry through the kitchen door.

As he cautiously made his way through the house, his path lit only by his flashlight, the policeman could see no signs of a struggle. Everything was in place, giving no clues as to what had happened.

But as he climbed the stairs to the second floor, the beam of light fell on an object on the floor. Small, and round. At first, the policeman couldn't tell what it was, but as he looked closer, he realized to his horror that it was an eyeball.

It became clear to the policeman that more horrors were to come, and he called down to Monsieur Lancelin not to come any further into the house.

As he continued to climb the stairs, the officer stumbled upon the bodies of Madame and Genevieve Lancelin. Or rather, he assumed it was them, as their faces had been smashed with such ferocity that they were unrecognizable. Both women had had their eyes removed, and Madame Lancelin's eyeballs were discovered in the folds of the scarf she was wearing.

The officers were aware that in addition to the Lancelins, there were two maids living in the house. Assuming the bodies they had just discovered had been slaughtered by a madman, they climbed the second flight of stairs to the attic, fearing that they would also find the mutilated bodies of Christine and

Léa. They were also mindful of the fact that the murderer, or murderers, might still be in the house.

The door to the maids' room was locked from the inside, and the gendarme could see candlelight flickering from within. Calls to the girls to open the door were futile, so the officers broke down the door, and entered the small attic room.

Christine and Léa Papin were huddled up in bed together, having carefully removed their blood stained clothes and washed their bodies, before putting on clean bedclothes and climbing into bed together.

Next to the bed was a blood soaked hammer.[15]

What Happened Next

The sisters were taken for questioning. Christine was unapologetic in her admission of guilt, explaining matter-of-factly what had happened when the Lancelin women had returned home. Describing the moment that Madame Lancelin lost her temper over the iron, Christine continued:

"Then I rushed down to the kitchen and went to fetch a hammer and a knife, and with both instruments my sister and I fought on our two mistresses, we stabbed [their] heads with a knife, Struck with a pot of tin which was placed on a small table on the landing. We changed the instruments several times from one to the other, that is to say, that I passed to my sister the Hammer to strike and she passed the knife to us, we did the same with the tin pot, and the victims screamed, but I do not remember that they spoke a few words. I went to lock the door and closed the door of the vestibule as well. I closed these doors because I liked it better than the police who noticed our crime before our boss. Then my sister and I went to wash our hands...because we had them full of blood, then we got into our room, we took off our belongings which were stained with blood, we put on a bathrobe, we closed the door to our room, and we went to bed Both in the same bed. This is where you found us when you broke the door. I do not have any regrets or, in other words, I cannot tell you if I do not have any, I prefer to have the skin of my bosses rather than that they have mine or that of my sister. I did not premeditate my crime, I had no hatred towards them, but I do not accept the gesture that Madame Lancelin had for me this evening."

Léa refused to give any account of the evening's events, only to say that she agreed with everything Christine had said, adding:

"Everything [my] sister told you is accurate, the crimes happened exactly as she told you. My role in this case is absolutely the one she told you. I struck as much as she did, and I assert that we had not premeditated to kill our patrons, the idea came to us instantly when we heard that Madame Lancelin reproached us. [Like] my sister I have no regret for the criminal act we have committed...like my sister, I prefer to have the skin of my bosses rather than those who have had our own."[16]

The Trial

The Papin sisters were brought to trial in September 1933. It was an event which was followed by people all over France, and police had to be drafted in to help control the crowds.

In the run-up to the trial, Christine's behavior became more and more disturbing. The sisters had been separated after their arrest, and Christine displayed sexually driven behavior, calling out for her sister and writhing around on the floor in a sexual manner. She also began to experience the same hallucinations she had while she was with the Lancelins, and on one occasion attempted to gouge her own eyes out, resulting in her being restrained in a straight jacket.

Following this incident, Christine recanted her statement, claiming responsibility for both murders, and saying that Léa had had nothing to do with either of them. Léa, however, continued to take responsibility for her part, and Christine's attempts to free her sister were dismissed at the trial.

The sisters were both found guilty of murder. Christine was sentenced to death by guillotine, while Léa, who had only been charged with the murder of Madame Lancelin, received a lighter sentence of ten years' hard labor, as the jury believed that she had been heavily influenced by her older sister.

Christine's sentence was later commuted to life imprisonment, but she did not fare well. Pining for her beloved Léa, Christine became deeply depressed and stopped eating. She was transferred to an asylum in Rennes, but her condition never improved and she died in 1937 of *cachexia* – literally wasting away.

Léa, on the other hand, fared much better. She kept her head down and did what was asked of her, and after eight years she was released on good behavior. Extraordinarily, she settled in Nantes with her mother, Clémence, where she assumed the name of Marie and gained employment as a chambermaid.[17]

Léa

In September 1966, an article ran in the newspaper *France-Soir*. A journalist had tracked Léa down and interviewed her. Although the article was factually incorrect, and somewhat moralizing, it gave readers a glimpse into the madness that had taken hold of the youngest Papin sister.

"I do what I can to keep my room simple so that my sister, who watches me from above (because I'm certain she is in Paradise), doesn't laugh at me. I pray for her. I pray for our mother who lived with me until she died. To help me, she said...and all at once I didn't pray anymore. Christine watches me. She is always beautiful and young. She smiles as in the old days: with irony! I come apart, I shrivel up, I sweat from fear, I faint...And there's a trunk in my room."

She talked about her work at the hotel, and the fear she felt every time she made a mistake - of the young chambermaids who worked with her, and the teasing they bestowed upon her.

But her last words to the journalist showed her lack of grasp on reality and the sad delusion she had created for herself.

"When I don't have to work anymore, I want to become Sister Marie, at Bon Pasteur, in Le Mans. I've been saving for it. At Bon Pasteur, one of my older sisters is a nun. I'll go back to her..."[18]

THE SUNSET STRIP KILLER: The True Story of Carol Bundy

Jessi Gaines

Born Carol Mary Peters on August, 26, 1942, Carol Bundy's childhood, much like her adulthood, was spent pursuing a desperate need for attention and validation. Bundy's ability to idealize or overlook any unpleasantness made her a perfect victim for manipulators and abusers looking for a potential victim – a talent she picked up early on to deal with the abuses of her parents, Charles and Gladys Peters.

Bundy's memories of her childhood are happy ones – Christmases where her parents refused to let their three children miss out on the special holiday because of a lack of money, or her father's attempt to convince her that the tooth fairy had visited overnight, using a doll's feet to leave footprints through Bundy's bedroom. Bundy's mother worked as a hairdresser, but had previously been a stand-in for tap-dancer Ruby Keeler – and Bundy remembered her as a woman who exuded beauty and glamour.

Bundy, on the other hand, was awkward and unattractive, leading her mother to begin treating her as though she didn't even exist. When she was eight, Bundy came home to a locked door, and no matter how much she cried or begged her mother to let her in, Gladys refused – stating that Bundy was not her daughter. Eventually, Charles persuaded Gladys to let the girl in, but even though Bundy was allowed back into the home, her mother ignored her completely.

However, Charles was not without reproach. Gladys, who had a tendency to beat the children relentlessly with a belt, wasn't permitted to hit Bundy or her siblings – but Charles was fond of using physical abuse to assert his dominance. While Bundy remembers her father's beatings as fitting to the severity of the offense, Charles was an alcoholic who used Gladys' death as an excuse to move his assaults on his daughters from physical to sexual.

For eight months, Charles molested both Bundy and her sister Vicky, telling the girls it was their responsibility to "take their mother's place in his bed." Although Vicky maintains that the sexual abuse continued until Charles remarried, Bundy can only recall one instance where her father molested her – and described him as a good man, who loved her.

When Charles remarried, though, he began abusing Bundy more often – beating her, degrading her, humiliating her. He told her she was stupid and fat, and even that he wanted to kill her and the rest of the family – but he'd only gotten as far as the cat before his new wife had taken away his gun. After staying in foster homes, with their grandmother, and with an uncle, the girls were brought back to live with their father in California.

Desperate measures

At this point, Bundy was willing to do anything to get away from her father – and at the age of 17, she married a 56-year-old alcoholic to try and escape the abuse. Bundy had discovered how to use her sexuality and large breasts to seduce men and receive the attention she so desperately needed – but she was unwilling to prostitute herself for her new husband. When she left him, Bundy took up with another older man, a 32-year-old writer named Richard Geis.

With encouragement from Geis, who appreciated her wit and intelligence, Bundy embarked on a brief but somewhat successful writing career. However, after her father hung himself in 1962, Bundy sought comfort through sexual encounters with women. Bouncing frequently between male lovers and female lovers, Bundy was unable to find a reliable source of the attention she needed, so she eventually returned to Geis and the couple moved to Oregon.

Still, Bundy would occasionally let other men pay her for sex. Instead of urging her to seek counseling, Geis agreed to support Bundy while she attended nursing school in Santa Monica – he would pay for her education as long as she kept her grades up. In fact, Bundy was named class valedictorian when she completed the program in 1968.

It was in nursing school that Bundy met her next husband, Grant. Their relationship started off well, and continued to be relatively stable until the birth of their first son – but then, Bundy claimed, he started beating and belittling her. By the time Bundy had given birth to their second son, her eyesight had deteriorated to the point where it looked like she may have to give up nursing. Grant was faced with the prospect of being saddled with the responsibility of caring for a blind wife, as well as their two children, and grew increasingly more violent.

Bundy escaped the abusive marriage and took her two boys to a womens' shelter in 1979, where she stayed for two weeks before finding a small apartment in Van Nuys. The managers of the Valerio Gardens apartment building, Jeanette and John "Jack" Murray, took pity on the poor single mother, and Jack was frequently called on to help Bundy with issues at the apartment. Despite her husband's established pattern of cheating, Jeanette wasn't concerned about the 36-year-old month – Bundy was overweight with short brown hair, a stark contrast to Murray's typical blonde, long-legged mistresses.

The object of her affection

The kindness she saw from Murray led Bundy to develop a crush on her landlord, who took her to the Social Security office so she could receive disability payments and even to the optometrist, to get her fitted for a pair of glasses to help the single mother return to work. Murray, for his part, enjoyed having a captive audience. Good looking, with a fantastic voice, Murray had come to America from Australia to pursue a career in music – but had been unable to make it as a performer thanks to his arrogant attitude.

The two found exactly what they needed in each other, and soon began a sexual relationship. Bundy's crush rapidly became an obsession, and she started coming up with more frequent excuses to have her landlord visit her property. Her infatuation for Murray convinced Bundy that he was in love with her, too – even though he told her it would be years before he would be able to leave his wife. Bundy was well-versed in the art of overlooking negative or painful thoughts and feelings, and continued to look for ways to strengthen the connection she saw with Murray.

Regularly, Bundy loaned her landlord money and bought him expensive gifts after she received the settlement from the sale of the house she'd owned with Grant. She also opened a joint safety deposit box with Murray, and made deposits to help him cover the expenses he said he was incurring as a result of his wife's alleged cancer treatments. Still, Murray wasn't giving Bundy the attention she craved, and she started up a brief affair with Jeanette's younger brother.

In an attempt to spend some time alone with her lover, Bundy arranged a weekend for her and Murray in Las Vegas – as a "reward" for all of his help, she said. However, after the couple checked in at the hotel and took in a show, Murray left Bundy alone for the remainder of the weekend while he gambled. He returned in time to fly back with Bundy, and, hurt and upset, Bundy forgot her suitcase in Murray's van.

When Jeanette showed up at Bundy's door with the forgotten suitcase, Bundy used the opportunity to try and bring her affair with Murray to his wife's attention – thinking Murray would then be forced to leave his wife and finally be with Bundy. During their discussion, Bundy learned that Jeanette never had cancer, and she immediately confronted Murray. While Bundy was initially angry to learn that the money she'd given him to pay for the treatments had actually been used to pay off Murray's van, he calmed her down by reassuring her that his intention was still to leave his wife and eventually be with Bundy. Eventually.

However, Bundy was losing her patience. On Christmas Day, when Murray didn't show up to spend any time with her and her children, she made the decision to take matters into her own hands. Bundy attempted to bribe Jeanette into leaving her husband – which Jeanette accepted, as long as this was Murray's desire, as well. Bundy left with the hope that later that evening, she and Murray would finally be able to start their life together. But when Murray came to talk to her after discussing the situation with his wife, he told Bundy to "stay out of his life," telling her there was "no way" he would let her break up his family.

Devastated, Bundy spent a few days licking her wounds, but still turned up three days later at Murray's favorite bar, the "Little Nashville Club." Murray regularly played music at the bar, but that night, he was simply enjoying himself off-stage, dancing with his wife. Heartbroken, Bundy felt her dream of a life with Murray slip further and further away – but caught the eye of an attractive blond gentleman, who she saw watching her from across the bar.

After an evening of dancing, Bundy was taken with the stranger from the bar. Rather than taking advantage of her promiscuity, this new man treated Bundy with respect – which made her feel like a true lady, cherished and appreciated. Charmed, Bundy felt like she and Doug Clark were made for each other, and was already looking forward to seeing him again when he dropped her off at home and promised to call on her soon.

A whirlwind romance

Doug Clark waited only a few days before calling Bundy and asking to see her again. Although Bundy preferred to keep her male callers away from her children, she relented when Clark suggested he come over for dinner – and was pleased to see that her boys took to him immediately. They played, cuddled, and Clark even tucked the boys in for bed before telling them that he would be spending the night with their mother. Bundy loved the way he took care of things, and was more than willing to give him complete control.

For the first time, Bundy made love with a partner who seemed truly interested in giving her pleasure, rather than just letting her do all the work. He was an affectionate lover, telling her over and over again how much he wanted her, how much he appreciated her, how smart and beautiful she was. This was all new to Bundy, and played right into her desperate need for validation.

The next morning, however, Bundy awoke to see Clark looking concerned and anxious – his landlady was causing him grief, he said, so would she mind terribly if he moved some of his things into her apartment? Enamoured, Bundy was eager to accommodate Clark's desires, even when he requested a pair of her panties – just so he could remember her, even when they were apart. Although she felt somewhat uncomfortable with it, Bundy gave her new lover a pair of her large, cotton panties, which he promptly returned to her when he saw how big they were. Bundy was hurt, but she was still thrilled to have found such an attractive, caring, respectful man who was so interested in her.

Still, Clark's attentions weren't enough to tear Bundy away from Murray. After sending him several letters professing her deep, unwavering love for him, Bundy made another attempt to manipulate him away from his wife. This time, though, Murray refused to indulge Bundy's long-standing delusions, and told her it was finally time to move out of the building. Although reluctant, Bundy moved into a new apartment just three miles away – big enough for herself, her two sons, and her new lover.

After moving her furniture into the new suite, Murray left with his wife, but returned frequently to have sex with Bundy or persuade her into lending him more money. Not surprisingly, Murray and Clark disliked each other immediately, which Bundy interpreted as jealousy – a sign of their love for her. She told Clark how Murray had exploited her affection for him by asking for loans and gifts. Enraged, Clark demanded that Bundy cut him off immediately. She agreed, but kept the joint account open.

The perfect couple

Clark's anger over Murray's mistreatment of Bundy encouraged her enough to overlook the fact that her new live-in boyfriend wasn't covering his share of the rent, bills, or food. Bundy's new job at Valley Medical Centre, where she was now working as a vocational nurse, paid her more than enough to cover the expenses – and Bundy was content to take care of everything, as long as Clark continued to provide her with his love and affection.

Unfortunately, Clark was having a hard time keeping this up. He was proving himself to be just as self-absorbed as Murray – talking constantly about himself and his needs, with no real interest in hearing about anything Bundy brought up. However, the couple grew closer together after Clark read an article about expressing true love by fulfilling each other's fantasies. Eagerly, Clark convinced Bundy to start opening up about her own sexual desires, and he began to do the same.

Clark's fantasies were dark, but Bundy was thrilled that he was sharing these intimate thoughts with her. Bundy had a budding interest in bondage and domination, and particularly enjoyed imagining herself as Clark's captured sex slave – although in his fantasy, this role was filled by some young girl. But Clark loved that Bundy's sexual limits seemed virtually non-existent, and he pushed to include even darker subject matter, even murder. If she loved him, Clark told Bundy, she "should be willing to kill for him." Desperate to please him, she assured him that she would.

Their relationship was inconsistent. Clark would regularly disappear for hours and even days at a time, withdrawing from Bundy and drawing out her deepest insecurities. When he would eventually return, Bundy would be so relieved and happy to see him that she would say anything to convince him to stay. She also continued to react with pleasure and excitement as Clark's nighttime fantasy sharing grew increasingly sordid and graphic – even when he told her details of an ex-girlfriend's experiences with necrophilia.

A near escape

Bundy's penchant for promiscuity led her to browse personal ads occasionally, especially during Clark's frequent absences. When a posting from a well-to-do studio executive named Art Pollinger caught her eye, Bundy bravely responded to the ad. Pollinger weighed nearly four hundred pounds, but he was looking for a wife and thought Bundy a worthy prospect. Her tried-and-true method of using her past abuses to entice new lovers paid off again, and Pollinger – who genuinely enjoyed Bundy's company and thought her to be an intelligent and interesting woman – encouraged her to cut ties with Murray.

Eventually, after some persuading, Bundy allowed Polliger to drive her to the bank, where she withdrew the money she had left in the joint safety-deposit box she'd opened with Murray. Nearly $6000 was missing, and withdrawal slips were signed with Murray's name, but Bundy continued to defend Murray's deceit. Still, she took the rest of the money and put it in a chequing account where Murray would be unable to access it.

Despite Pollinger's genuine affection and desire to share his life with Bundy, the two ended up parting ways. Bundy was used to the emotional abuse she had endured in her previous relationships, and couldn't be satisfied in a healthy relationship.

Red flags

After having surgery to restore her sight, Bundy was excited at the prospect of purchasing a new car – and so was Clark, who had selected a blue 1973 Buick station wagon. Even though the car was large and difficult for Bundy to drive, since her peripheral vision was severely limited, she bought it anyway. She was desperate to give Clark everything he asked for – even guns, which he said she should have for protection. From a pawn shop in Van Nuys, Clark selected two .25 calibre Raven automatics, which Bundy was more than willing to pay for and register in her own name.

By now, Bundy's older son was starting to notice how Clark dominated his mother, and begged her to kick him out. Instead of taking her child's concern to heart, however, Bundy refused to acknowledge Clark's abuse – choosing to lash out at her son, instead. Clark and Bundy regularly beat him, and once, Clark even graphically detailed how he could kill the boy – with Bundy's son right next to him. Rather than defending her child, though, Bundy merely watched as Clark's behaviour grew more and more violent.

The couple had even stopped having sex, as Clark informed Bundy that she was too unattractive to arouse him anymore. Desperate to please him, Bundy began accompanying Clark as he picked up prostitutes from the Sunset Strip, and would watch from the backseat while he forced the usually young women to service him orally.

According to former FBI Special Agent Robert R. Hazelwood, who worked with the Behavioural Sciences Unit, men like Clark employ a specific process that can turn vulnerable women into accomplices. After identifying a woman like Bundy, desperate for attention, they use seduction techniques to reshape the woman's sexual norms – even if the woman is initially disturbed or frightened.

"These men have the ability to recognize vulnerable women and manipulate them," Hazelwood said. "The behaviour gets reinforced with attention and affection, gifts and excitement. Eventually, they are doing things that isolate them and further lower their self-esteem. All they have is this guy, so they cooperate."

Clark had plenty of experience in charming women enough to get them to do whatever he wanted, but although he had tried, he had been unable to find a suitable woman to replace Bundy. None of the other women he dated were as willing to indulge his dark sexual fantasies as Bundy was, so despite his mounting contempt for her, Clark continued to live with Bundy on and off. Bundy reassured herself that even though Clark had other girlfriends, she was the one he shared his intimate fantasies with – his feelings for her, she thought, must be deeper.

More than just fantasies

When Clark showed up at her apartment in late April, 1980, covered in blood, Bundy realized his murderous tendencies had taken a step beyond his imagination. Although Bundy chose to believe a fabricated tale Clark wove where he'd been attacked by a girl's boyfriend, the real story came out when a young prostitute named Charlene identified Doug Clark as the man who had stabbed her repeatedly with a knife after picking her up and requesting oral sex. She had been lucky to escape alive.

Bundy's suspicions mounted further when she discovered a bag of clothes and a blanket in the backseat of the Buick – covered in blood. When she confronted Clark, he told her the same kind of graphic story of sexual perversion that she'd become accustomed to hearing – only this time, the story was real.

Clark had spotted two young runaways, 15-year-old Cindy and her 16-year-old stepsister, Gina, at a bus stop. After picking them up and demanding Cindy give him oral sex, he told Bundy that he shot both girls until they were dead and then drove with the bodies to a garage he rented in Burbank. Once inside the garage, Clark said he dragged the bodies onto an old mattress and proceeded to perform acts of necrophilia on their corpses.

That night, after confessing to Bundy, Clark returned to the garage with a camera borrowed from one of his other girlfriends. After playing with the bodies again, he wrapped them in the blanket and dumped them in a ditch off the Ventura Freeway. Bundy was thrilled that he'd chosen to confess this activity to her, instead of any of the other women he was involved with.

Still, Bundy felt compelled to report the murders to the Van Nuys police. When she called the department the night after Clark's confession, she told the officer that she believed her boyfriend had committed the crime. Although Bundy told the officer some details of the case, she wasn't taken seriously, and when the call was disconnected, they assumed the "crank caller" had just hung up.

Clark started telling Bundy about other murders he claimed to have committed, including the killing of a man named Vic Weiss and the slaying of a young prostitute identified by police as teenage runaway Marnett Comer. Their relationship had become completely centered around Clark's murderous desires and Bundy's desperate need for his attention. Even though he no longer made any attempt to flatter or even be kind to Bundy, Clark had her completely under his control.

Only a few months later, at the end of June, Bundy accompanied Clark on what would be their first murder together. Cathy, who the couple picked up off Hollywood's Highland Avenue, looked about 17 years old, and agreed to perform oral sex on Clark for $30. Bundy, watching from the backseat, passed Clark the gun when Cathy failed to get him erect. He shot her, and as she lay dying with her head in Bundy's lap, Clark drove the car out into the country. Cathy was left along a gravel road near the Magic Mountain amusement park.

The very next night, Clark came home and told Bundy of another killing. He'd spotted three prostitutes working together, and convinced one of them, Exxie Wilson, to get in the Buick. After killing her and cutting off her head, Clark realized the other two women might be able to identify him if Wilson's body was found, so he went back and picked up one of the other prostitutes, later identified as Karen Jones. Clark left Jones' body near the Burbank Studios, and, after giving up on finding the third girl, returned to Bundy's apartment with Wilson's head.

They kept the head in the freezer for a few days, and Clark told Bundy how he would take it into the shower with him and push his penis into the open mouth. Eventually, Bundy cleaned the head and put it in an ornate treasure chest, which they dumped near the Studio City Sizzler where Clark had left the rest of Wilson's body. The chest was discovered almost immediately, and the relationship between Bundy and Clark grew even more strained.

The unraveling

In an attempt to gain back Clark's affections, Bundy agreed to participate in a three-way sexual relationship involving their 11-year-old neighbour, who Clark had been molesting for months. Since news of the Sunset Strip murders was spreading, prostitutes were hesitant to work alone, and it was increasingly difficult for Clark and Bundy to find anyone willing to get in their car.

Police were holding press conferences where they discussed evidence that seemed to link the cases – leading them to believe this may be the work of a serial killer. It was even suspected that the killer lived in the area, Detective Sergeant John Helvin stated to the press, "but we don't know for sure."

The stress of this ongoing investigation and Clark's lack of interest in her led Bundy to a desperate suicide attempt, and when she woke up alone at a hospital in Burbank, Bundy called Murray to come pick her up.

Bundy was willing to do anything to reignite Murray's sexual interest in her, so she started bringing her young neighbour for him to fondle. When that still wasn't enough, Bundy turned to her reliable method of playing the victim to gain her lover's sympathy – she told Murray about the murders. Although Murray didn't threaten to tell the police, Bundy knew she couldn't keep him alive. Besides, this was her opportunity to prove to Clark that she would kill for him.

On August 3, 1980, Murray climbed into the back of his van, anticipating oral sex. Instead, Bundy shot him in the head twice and stabbed him in the back half a dozen times. When she realized the bullets in Murray's head would help the police identify her gun, she cut his head off and put it in a plastic bag, eventually dumping it in a trash can near Griffith Park.

The rest of his body was found just days later, left in his van in the parking lot at the Little Nashville club. Police began questioning regulars at the club, including Murray's wife, Jeanette. Bundy was brought down to the police station and gave detectives her version of the alibi she had already discussed with Clark, which included a detailed description of a man she had supposedly sold her two guns to.

But none of this was enough for Clark, who refused to accept any of the blame for the rapidly deteriorating situation. He told Bundy that he was moving out, and left her alone while he went out to spend time with a new girlfriend. After briefly speaking to her mother-in-law and her sons, Bundy called Geis and told him about the murders. The next morning, after being berated by Clark as she drove him to work, Bundy confessed to a co-worker about the crime spree. By the end of the day, both Clark and Bundy were arrested in relation to the series of Sunset Strip murders.

According to police commander William Booth, evidence gathered during the investigation of Murray's death, along with the information collected during the ongoing investigation into the Sunset Strip murders, let them to Clark and Bundy. Bundy would end up telling the police graphic details about each murder, admitting that she thought killing was "really fun to do."

The end of the Sunset Strip

Despite the mountains of evidence connecting Clark to the killings, he continued to claim his innocence – even after he was found guilty on six counts of murder and sentenced to death. Bundy, who had initially entered a plea of "not guilty by reason of insanity," managed to avoid a similar fate by pleading guilty to her two counts of murder. She was sentenced to two consecutive terms of 25 years to life, with an added two years for using a firearm illegally.

Until her death in 2003, Bundy fought desperately to prove Clark's innocence – even as he attempted to put all the blame on her.

CYNTHIA COFFMAN

James Marlow and Cynthia Coffman were a troubled couple who were convicted of murdering five people during a deadly rampage that spanned multiple states. The last two victims, 20-year old Corrina Novis and 19-year old Lynell Murray were kidnapped and found strangled and sodomized, and the murderous pair were found guilty of the crimes. Whereas both Marlow and Coffman received the death penalty for Novis' death, Marlow received a second death sentence for Murray's while Coffman was sentence to life without the possibility of parole in Murray's murder. Both defendants sought to shift the onus of blame to the other with Marlow claiming it was Coffman's idea to kill the girls while he only wanted to rob them and Coffman alleging that she was the victim of battered women's syndrome. Neither ploy was successful as the pair were convicted across the board for robbery, kidnapping, sodomy, and murder. Coffman has the distinction of being the first woman sentenced to death in California following the state's reinstatement of the death penalty in 1977.

Early Lives

James

James Gregory Marlow was born on 11 May 1956 in Ohio but raised in Kentucky; the son of a beautiful but amoral hillbilly woman named Doris who virtually ensured that her son would grow up completely dysfunctional. Throughout his childhood, Marlow witnessed abuse, neglect, drug use, and sex courtesy of his mother who often prostituted herself in front of him. She gave birth to another child, Veronica Koppers, in 1959 and would frequently leave her children alone or with neighbors. Marlow eventually went to live with his father, Arnold, who would beat him severely and lock him in cabinets and, subsequently, went back to his mother's house. Despite the abuse and her horrific behavior, Marlow loved his mother dearly. So much, in fact, that when he was 13 years old his mother shot him up with drugs and seduced him. During interviews Marlow openly admitted to having had sexual relations with his mother on several occasions and that he didn't know it was wrong. He loved his mother so much and thought it was normal. Experts assert that Marlow suffered from traumatic bonding in which a traumatic event—his mother's seduction—created a dysfunctional yet significant bond from which he could not escape.

By the time Marlow was 16 years old he was living alone in California and married his first of three wives. Thanks to his mother, Marlow developed a severely skewed view of women. When she died in a trailer fire he was completely distraught and "took on the sins of his parents" by turning to a life of crime and violence. In one incident when he was still a teenager, Marlow was talking to one of his cousin's girlfriend, Darlene Miller, who he—one day while driving her to a nearby convenience store—pulled over in front of an old, abandoned house and forced Miller into the house where he beat and hogtied her, and then locked her in a closet. Over a span of three days Marlow would repeatedly beat, rape, and sodomize Miller. She escaped and ran to a neighbor's house—a house that Marlow had recently burglarized. Police were called and Marlow was arrested and after a tearful pretrial interview wherein he tearfully detailed the issues with his mother, he was sent to a drug rehabilitation center in 1975 for seven months and, soon after his release in 1976 was rearrested for being under the influence. Marlow was eventually imprisoned for burglary, robbery, and drug charges and was ultimately sentenced to California's notorious Folsom Prison in 1980. It was here that Marlow—not unlike the majority of inmates—got heavily tattooed with one—a howling wolf on his right side—earning him the nickname of the Folsom Wolf.

Prior to meeting Coffman, Marlow had an extensive criminal record. On 5 November 1979 in Upland, California, Marlow and his friend Allen Smallwood, who were both heroin addicts, assaulted Jeffrey Johnson in his apartment, searched it for non-existent drugs, then took Johnson downstairs—by knifepoint—to the Liesches' apartment where they searched the second apartment for more non-existent drugs, tied up the residents—Lori and Kathy—with electrical cords, and stole some cash they had found.

The following day, Marlow entered an Upland, California, leather goods store owned by Joanne Gilligan who was helping a customer, said he had a gun in his pocket and ordered them to lie on the floor, and then robbed the register of cash and took two jackets.

At approximately 10:00 a.m. on 20 November that same year, Gertrude Smith and Wilson Lee were working at an Ontario, California, methadone clinic when Marlow and Smallwood entered brandishing a sawed-off shotgun and pistol, respectively, and demanded methadone which they were told was locked in a safe. Another employee opened the safe and the two left with methadone that had a street value of $10,000. When Marlow was finally arrested on 26 November he had a bottle of methadone in his jacket and had the shotgun wrapped in a shirt.

Cynthia

Cynthia Lynn Haskins was born on 19 January 1962 in St. Louis, Missouri. From the beginning her life was to be difficult. Born with a double hernia that precluded her mother from holding her, Cynthia never experienced the necessary mother-infant bonding so crucial for healthy adjustment. As a result, she suffered from a crucial lack of empathy and a driving propensity to seek affections elsewhere. Cynthia's father left when she was three years old and her mother—who had aspirations of becoming a singer—allegedly tried to give her and her brothers Robbie and Jeff away several times during their childhood; with Jeff eventually given up for adoption. Cynthia was frequently "farmed out" to relatives that made her become more rebellious, defiant, and reckless. By the time she was a sophomore in high school, Cynthia was already experimenting with marijuana and methamphetamine with her new friends.

Her mother remarried a successful businessman named Bill Maender with whom Cynthia did not get along. Truancy, rebelliousness, and ultimately not wanting to live by her stepfather's rules caused Cynthia to run away at age 17 to her boyfriend's, Ron Coffman, house. When Cynthia returned three months later, pregnant, abortion was not an option for her devout parents and she refused to give the baby up for adoption, so she was forced into a loveless marriage with Coffman. The marriage quickly deteriorated and Ron filed for divorce because of Cynthia's infidelities, drug use, and poor housekeeping while Cynthia accused him of physical and emotional abuse and infidelity. Cynthia then worked in a carburetor factory to take care of her son, Joshua. She ultimately abandoned Joshua after two years, leaving him with her ex-husband (allegedly intending to get him back after she got settled) although later, when she and Marlow were committing their heinous crimes she suggested that Marlow kill her ex-husband and ex-in-laws (who had legal custody of Joshua) so she could regain custody of her son. While on death row Coffman exchanges letters with her son who believes his mother to be in prison for drug-related charges. She has stated in interviews that she wants to be the one to tell him the truth someday.

There is much speculation that Coffman had antisocial personality disorder which is characterized by little regard for right and wrong or the feelings of others. Further, those with the chronic disorder tend to manipulate, antagonize, and treat others with a callous indifference, are very prone to violate the law, are easily angered, lie, behave impulsively and/or violently, and use and abuse drugs and alcohol—all without remorse or guilt. Coffman exhibited a number of these traits, many of which worsened once she began her relationship with Marlow.

In May 1984 Coffman left home with a girlfriend and journeyed west where she wound up in Page, Arizona, and moved in with her new boyfriend, Doug Huntley. The lovebirds moved to Barstow, California where Huntley had some friends. He secured employment in construction while she was a bartender and waitress and sold methamphetamines on the side. One evening they were involved in an altercation outside of a convenience store in which Coffman pulled a gun on several men who were hassling her boyfriend and this resulted in both Huntley and Coffman being arrested and jailed. While Coffman was released after a few days, Huntley became cellmates with Marlow. Huntley told Marlow all about Coffman which intrigued Marlow who, upon his release soon thereafter, showed up at Coffman's apartment. It was love at first sight as Coffman reminded Marlow of his mother and Marlow was every bit the bad boy to whom Coffman was attracted. Even after Huntley was released, Marlow, Coffman, and he remained friends until Huntley returned to prison in June of that year.

A Dangerous Partnership

Marlow and Coffman began their contentious, dysfunctional, and murderous relationship amidst drugs and violence; her former boyfriend Huntley all but forgotten. In June 1986 Marlow had Coffman drive him to Fontana, California, and to his cousin Debbie Schwab's house where he purchased methamphetamines. A few days later they went to Newberry Springs and stayed with some of Marlow's friends, Steve and Karen Schmitt. Marlow told Coffman that he was a hit man, a martial arts expert, and a White supremacist who had murdered African American while in prison. It was during this time that Coffman saw Marlow turn into "Wolf"—his angry, violent alter-ego. Coffman testified in court that Marlow would beat her and then apologize and things would be fine again for a while. This is classic cycle-of-violence behavior central to most domestic violence cases. At this point Marlow allegedly took Coffman's address book that had her mother's and son's addresses and refused to give it back to her; essentially holding it as a carrot just out of reach to get her to do what he wanted.

They traveled across the country visiting Marlow's relatives in Kentucky and Tennessee. He had told Marlow that his father had recently died and left him some land in Kentucky and that they could get her son and live as a family there. First, however, they needed a vehicle and Marlow allegedly pressured Coffman to steal her friend's red Nissan pickup truck that Marlow and friend Paul Donner painted black. Marlow and Coffman jumped in the truck, stole some license plates from an off road vehicle outside of Newberry Springs, California, and headed east.

In Woodland Park, Colorado, Marlow called Gene Kelly, a contractor who constructed microwave telephone relay towers and who Marlow had met when he was a temporary laborer for him a few years back, to see if he needed any help in Colorado at the time. (There is some discrepancy in the available literature with respect to this individual being named Gene Kelly or Elmer Lutz; however, the actual criminal case against the defendants state Kelly). Kelly told him that he didn't have any work at the time but that he would have some work in Atlanta, Georgia, in a few weeks. The couple went to Colorado Springs for a couple of days and then to St. Louis to see Coffman's grandmother. They arrived on 2 July and Coffman called her mother who was less than happy to hear from her. The couple continued their journey east.

In Pine Knot, Kentucky, Marlow called his cousin Donald "Lardo" Lyons and both he and Coffman stayed with him for several days. Marlow had expected a modest inheritance from his grandmother Lena Walls with whom Marlow and his sister Veronica were close when they were younger; however, by the time Marlow reached Kentucky there was nothing left for him. Needing money, Marlow agreed to meet with Lardo's friend Shannon "Killer" Compton and the trio discussed how a local man named Greg "Wildman" Hill was going to be testifying in court against a mutual acquaintance and that Hill should "be silenced." They arranged for Compton to give Lyons a sum of money of which Lyons would give $5,000 to Marlow to get rid of Hill.

The next day, 7 July 1986, Lyons gave Marlow a .22 caliber pistol and at 5:00 a.m. Marlow and Coffman got into their stolen black Nissan pickup and drove to Hill's house. For most of the day the two of them parked relatively close and surveilled his house, did drugs, and engaged in sex. Finally, Marlow ordered Coffman to take off her shirt and bra and to tie a bandana across her chest like a bikini top and to knock on Hill's door to elicit help for her "stalled" truck. Hill agreed and tucked his own pistol inside his jeans' waistband. At the truck, when Marlow came after Hill with his own gun, Hill drew his and after an ensuing struggle Hill's gun went off, mortally wounding him with a bullet to the head. Marlow wiped his fingerprints off Hill's gun and left it at the scene.

Lyons kept true to his word giving Marlow the $5,000 "fee" for his "hit." The next day Marlow gave the stolen Nissan to a relative and spent $3,000 on a Harley Davidson; something he wanted for a very long time. On 11 July 1986 Marlow and Coffman had a "biker" wedding atop a Marlow's new Harley. Witnesses alleged that Coffman's face was bruised and scratched from a recent beating Marlow have given her. Such violence was not an isolated incident. In fact, one time while Marlow was assaulting Coffman one of his acquaintances asked what he was doing and Marlow dislocated his arm. As a result, nobody else ever intervened when Marlow was in one of his rages against Coffman. She said that when Marlow turns into "Wolf" his voice becomes monotone and his eyes and facial expression changes—that he becomes a completely different and violent person.

Marlow ended up giving the Nissan to a friend and purchasing a 1970's Cadillac to continue their journey to Atlanta and a job with Kelly. Marlow did manage to work for four days before an incident wherein he, Coffman, and a group of coworkers went out for dinner but which turned into Marlow beating Coffman outside of the restaurant and inside the vehicle, seemingly because she assisted some men with a stuck ball at a pool table. Back at the hotel where they were staying, Marlow was not finished with Coffman. He asked her for her scissors and then queried, "Your hair or your eye?" Horrified, Coffman said her hair and Marlow cut it as short as he could with her small scissors. He then taunted her that he would pierce her eye as well before making her strip naked and forcing her to stand outside the hotel room for several minutes. He then let her back into the room where he forcibly sodomized her. The following morning Marlow found a check from Kelly that had been slid under the door for his four days of work. After a few more days of going on "pot hunts" and unsuccessfully attempting a burglary in July 1986 in Whitley County, Kentucky, the couple left and headed back to Arizona.

In Arizona, Marlow and Coffman burglarized her former boyfriend Doug Huntley's parents' house and stole their safe that contained ten silver dollars—which they kept—and some papers. They buried the safe in the dessert. The next stop was back in Newberry Springs, California, where the couple stole two rings from the Schmitts; one they pawned for cash and the other they traded for methamphetamines.

Returning to Fontana, California, in early October 1986, Marlow and Coffman stayed with his cousins, the Schwabs. During their visit Marlow tattooed "Property of Folsom Wolf" on Coffman's buttocks and the word "W-O-L-F" and some lightning bolts on her ring finger as a wedding band. They then spent some time with Marlow's friends Rita Robbeloth and her son Curtis, and then with his sister, her husband Paul Koppers, and his brother, Steve. During this time Coffman alleges that after asking for an equal share of the methamphetamine they had, Marlow became angry and beat her, threatened to kill her, forced her to consume pills he said were cyanide, extinguished a cigarette on her face, and stabbed her in the leg. The pair then went to stay with another of Marlow's friends, Richard Drinkhouse.

The Crimes

On 11 October 1986 they were linked to the death of 32-year old Sandra Neary of Costa Mesa, California who never returned from a quick trip to a local ATM machine to withdraw some money. Her car was found in a nearby parking lot and her body was later found on 24 October by some hikers near Corona, California. Their next victim was 35-year old Pamela Simmons. She was reported missing in Bullhead City, Arizona, on 28 October. Her abandoned car was found by the local police department and the theory was that she was also abducted while withdrawing money from an ATM.

Corinna Novis

On 7 November, 20-year old Corinna Novis vanished from a First Interstate Bank parking lot near a shopping mall in Redlands, California, in broad daylight. Alone, she was driving her white Honda CR-X and when she failed to make her manicure appointment at her friend Terry Davis' salon, and then failed to make a 7:00 p.m. pizza date with other friends, she was reported missing. That same day, Marlow and Coffman were at the Redlands Mall visiting his sister Koppers who worked at a restaurant and were supposed to pick her up from work; however, Marlow gave his sister back her keys, telling her that they already had a ride. Coffman, clad in a dress, and Marlow, in a suit and tie, probably seemed rather innocuous to Novis when they asked her for a ride. Earlier that day Marlow had told Coffman that they needed to "get a girl" but Coffman alleged that she did not know that Marlow intended to kill her.

At approximately 7:30 p.m., they took Novis to Marlow's friend Richard Drinkhouse's house who was home alone recovering from a motorcycle accident at the time. Coffman took their hostage into the bedroom after telling Drinkhouse they needed to use the bathroom. Marlow told Drinkhouse that Coffman was trying to get her ATM pin number so they could "rob" her bank account. Drinkhouse didn't appreciate their intrusion into his house to which Marlow assured Drinkhouse that that there wouldn't be any witnesses because how could Novis talk to anyone "if she's under a pile of rocks"? Soon thereafter, Marlow's sister Koppers showed up and she and Coffman left the house to go to a nearby 7-Eleven while Marlow cautioned Drinkhouse not to leave and then returned to the bedroom where Novis was. After Coffman returned, she went into the bedroom to change clothes and after what sounded like the shower running the three of them emerged from the bedroom—Novis' and Marlow's hair were wet (Coffman testified that she had nothing to do with "what went on in the shower"). Novis was handcuffed and had duct tape over her mouth. They left the house and Drinkhouse testified that he never saw Novis again.

The next day, Marlow and Coffman asked Drinkhouse if he wanted to buy an answering machine. Novis' employer Jean Cramer, went to check on her the morning of 10 November when she uncharacteristically failed to appear at work and didn't call. She noticed Novis' car was missing, her front door was ajar, and her bedroom was in disarray. There was no evidence of forced entry and Novis' typewriter and answering machine were missing. On 7 November Koppers sold Novis' answering machine to a friend in exchange for a half-gram of methamphetamine who sold it to someone else and the Redlands Police Department ultimately recovered it. The next day, Harold Brigham who owned the Sierra Jewelry and Loan in Fontana testified that Coffman pawned Novis' typewriter using the victim's identification.

Back at the Robbeloths' house Coffman said Marlow changed clothes and tried to access money from Novis' account at a local First Interstate Bank; however, the PIN number she gave them was incorrect. The following day they ransacked Novis' apartment, found her PIN number, stole her money, pawned the typewriter they stole, disposed of Novis' belongings and then returned to Drinkhouse's house. On 12 November Marlow found out that his sister was in police custody and he and Coffman drove to Big Bear to get rid of Novis' car. They checked into the Bavarian Lodge using a credit card from another victim, Lynell Murray. They abandoned Novis' car on a dirt road south of Santa's Village which was approximately a quarter mile off of Highway 18 in the area. Coffman's fingerprints were found on the license plate, hood, and ashtray while Marlow's prints were found on the hood. The two then proceeded to walk along Big Bear Boulevard clad only in bathing suits despite the chilly weather; the stolen clothes that they had been wearing were discarded along with the handcuffs used on Novis. Receipts for clothing purchased by Marlow and Coffman were found in the clothing's pockets. The .22 caliber pistol the couple owned was in Coffman's purse.

Novis' body was discovered on 15 November lying face down in a shallow grave at a Fontana vineyard. She had been strangled and sodomized.

Dr. Gregory Reiber performed Novis' autopsy on 17 November and conclude that time of death was between five and ten days prior. Evidence of marks on her neck, injuries to her neck muscles, and thyroid cartilage fracture suggested death by strangulation; however, the presence of dirt in her throat also suggested possible suffocation. There was also biological evidence of sodomy.

Lynell Murray

On 12 November, 19-year old psychology student and Prime Cleaners dry cleaning shop clerk Lynell Murray failed to keep a date with her boyfriend, Robert Whitecotton, in Orange County. After noticing that the cleaners looked as though it had been burglarized and ransacked and that Murray's car was parked in the parking lot out back he called the police.

Murray had no idea that the previous day Marlow and Coffman saw her leaving work and that Marlow had commented that she would be "a good one to rob." The following evening at approximately 6:00 p.m., shortly before Murray was to leave work, one Lynda Schafer entered the cleaners and dropped of some clothes with Murray. Schafer would later testify that she saw Coffman "passionately embracing a man", later identified as Marlow, in an alley behind the cleaners.

At 6:30 p.m. that evening Coffman approached Linda Whitlake who was leaving her gym and asked for a ride to her motel, claiming that her car wouldn't start. After Whitlake noticed Marlow in Novis' white car with its hood up she changed her mind about giving them a ride. Coffman said that her boyfriend had decided to call the auto club instead and Whitlake left.

At 7:13 p.m. Coffman checked into room 307 of the Huntington Beach Inn under the name Lynell Murray and used Murray's credit card. At 8:19 p.m. a Bank of America branch in Corona del Mar recorded a balance inquiry into Murray's account and a subsequent withdrawal of $80 occurred, shortly followed by a $60 withdrawal, which left a balance of $4.41. Later that evening Coffman checked into the Compri Hotel in Ontario, California, with Murray's credit card. At midnight Marlow and Coffman ate dinner at the Denny's restaurant across from the hotel, which they paid for with Murray's credit card.

Murray's body would be discovered the following day at approximately 3:00 p.m. in room 307 at the Huntington Beach Inn. Her head was in the bathtub in six inches of water with it and her face bound with strips of towel. She was gagged. Her right arm was secured to her waist with a towel. Her right leg was atop the toilet and her left leg was on the floor. Her ankles looked to have been bound with duct tape as residue was evident. Her bra, nylons, and one earring were missing and she looked to have been raped and urinated on. She had also suffered pre-mortem blunt force trauma to the head, torso injuries, two black eyes, and leg bruising which were consistent with being beaten. The cause of death was determined to be ligature strangulation.

Police finally turned their attention to Marlow and Coffman after finding Novis' driver's license and checkbook in a Taco Bell takeout bag near a dumpster in Laguna Niguel along with papers with both Marlow's and Coffman's names on them. Marlow had attempted to dispose of this damning evidence but missed the dumpster. A statewide alert was issued for both Marlow and Coffman.

Arrest

On 14 November, police were dispatched to a Big Bear, California, mountain lodge after being alerted that Murray's credit card was being used to purchase clothes at a local sporting goods store. The owner of the lodge identified Marlow and Coffman as his latest guests. After finding the lodge empty, the 100-man posse discovered the suspects walking along a mountain road at approximately 3:00 p.m. They surrendered without incident, clad in clothing they had stolen from the dry cleaning shop where Murray had worked. A few hours later Coffman led police to Novis' body. One of the victim's earrings, a .22 caliber pistol and ammunition, credit card receipts with Murray's forged signature, and a Prime Cleaners paper bag with coins were found in Coffman's purse.

The Trial

Nearly three years later Marlow and Coffman would stand trial which commenced on 18 July 1989 in San Bernardino County. At several points throughout the proceedings motions for severance filed by both defendants were denied.

Among the overwhelming evidence were both defendants' fingerprints in Novis' car and that, as previously mentioned, Coffman was linked to the Fontana pawn shop where Novis' typewriter was pawned. In room 307 of the Huntington Beach Inn where Lynell Murray's body was found, a footprint on a bathmat by her body was consistent with Marlow's boots. The aforementioned Taco Bell bag with Novis' license and checkbook and documentation with Coffman's and Marlow's names was recovered. Credit card activity demonstrated where and when the defendants had used Murray's credit card. Additionally, the discarded suit jacket that Marlow had worn when they abducted Novis was found at the Bavarian Lodge and contained identification bearing Marlow's name, various single earrings presumed to be trophies from the murders, a blue ladies wallet, and the handcuffs used on Novis. Novis' vehicle was found near Santa's Village with license plates stolen from a vehicle that was at the Huntington Beach Inn and in a nearby trash can a maintenance worker found a pillowcase containing Murray's bra and laundry receipts from the cleaners where Murray had worked.

Coffman took the stand in her own behalf, painting Marlow to be an abusive man who was violent toward her and threatened both her and her son. She alleged that any violence directed toward the victims were perpetrated by

Marlow. With respect to Novis, Coffman testified that on the night of Novis' death, she had dropped Novis and Marlow off at the vineyard and was told to go purchase methamphetamines. Coffman alleges that she drove a short distance, stopped and smoked a cigarette, and then returned to "the sound of digging." Marlow returned to the vehicle alone, threw some items in the back of the car, and then started to beat her for driving away.

Coffman's attorney presented numerous witnesses who corroborated Coffman's allegations of Marlow's violence including Katherine Davis, one of Marlow's ex-wives, and her mother Marlene Boggs; Coffman's former employers in Arizona; Coffman's mother Carol Maender; and clinical psychologist Craig Rath who claimed that Coffman's relationship with Marlow was "precipitated by impaired bonding in her early life", that she was not malingering, and that she did not suffer from antisocial personality disorder.

In Marlow's defense, his sister Veronica Koppers testified about the abuse and neglect the two suffered at the hands of their mother and her father Wendell Hill; about how her father shot her mother and her mother stabbed her father seven times which prompted Doris to move to California in 1963; about visiting her mother at the Sybil Brand Institute for Women and the Frontera State Prison; about how Doris introduced her daughter to drugs much like she did with Marlow and taught her how to burglarize houses; and about the myriad drinking and drug parties hosted at their house. Several witnesses at the trial testified that Doris rarely even mentioned that she had children and paid them little attention when they were together. Despite Marlow claiming responsibility for the murder in Kentucky as well as Novis' and Murray's in California he tried to shift the majority of blame onto Coffman much as she attempted to do to him.

Throughout the trial, Coffman's legal team tried to utilize the "Patty Hearst" defense that she was brainwashed, starved, and the victim of battered women's syndrome who was subjected to frequent physical, emotional, and mental abuse. Once, she claimed, Marlow beat her with a motorcycle clutch plate bruising her face and another time kicked her with his steel-toed boots. She stated that she feared for both her life and that of her then-six-year old son. Coffman's side even presented an expert on battered women's syndrome; however, the jury apparently rejected such claims.

Other testimony suggested that Coffman was the true ringleader and cold, calculated murderess, being far more intelligent than Marlow who would do anything to keep her. At one point, prosecutor Robert Gannon asked Coffman whether her relationship with Marlow was more important than the lives of Corinna Novis and Lynell Murray to which she replied, "Yes."

Sentencing

Both defendants were convicted of the kidnapping, robbery, kidnapping for robbery, residential burglary, forcible sodomy, and murder of Novis and subsequently sentenced to death on 30 August 1989. Coffman became the first women sentenced to death in California since the state reinstated capital punishment in 1977; however, California's reputation as an overly liberal state makes it unlikely that Coffman will ever be put to death.

On 8 March 1992 Marlow received a second death sentence for Murray's murder while Coffman received a life without the possibility of parole sentence added to her death sentence, the former rather moot.

On 19 August 2004 the California Supreme Court unanimously upheld both Marlow's and Coffman's death sentences.

Post-conviction

There continues to be speculation as to whether Coffman controlled or was controlled by Marlow. In fact, while on Death Row, Marlow wrote *I Wish You Were Never Born*, a novel detailing Coffman's and his murderous spree (proceeds of the sale of his book are donated to help abused children). He asserts that their story in the popular media—including an episode of *Wicked Attractions*—was sensationalized and he wanted the truth to be known.

HUSBAND KILLER : THE TRUE STORY OF LARISSA SCHUSTER

ERIN EDWARDS

Larissa Leann Foreman was born January 1, 1960. She grew up on a farm near Clarence Missouri. By all accounts she had a happy childhood. She won first place at the Randolph pony show, her father, Charles, won first place in the men's division and Deeann, her mom, won second in the bareback for pleasure division. Her parents seemed to be very involved in her life. She excelled academically; she was athletic and went after what she wanted with everything she had. She was described as a 'go getter'.

Larissa graduated High school and went on to the University of Missouri Columbia to become a biochemist. She didn't come from a rich family so she would work as a nursing aide at Boone Hospital Center in Columbia Missouri. It's not known whether she liked her work as an aide, however she did like a nurse named Tim Schuster, and he liked her as well. She was electrifying and intoxicating, Tim was enthralled. They started dating after becoming friends and just hanging out together after work.

Finally, in 1982 Tim popped the question, and Larissa said yes. Between 1982 and the birth of their second child Tyler in 1990 there was a whirlwind of things happening. There was the wedding in '82, the birth of their first child, Kristin, and a move to sunny central California, Fresno to be exact.

In the beginning Tim managed the cardiology Department for St Agnes Medical Center. While Larissa worked for Pan Agricultural Laboratories. Larissa saw the company declining and thought it a good time to start her own company; Central California Research Lab. She was ambitious and worked long hours to make her company a success. Tim continued to work at St Agnes and be both Mom and Dad to their two children.

According to friends Bob and Mary Solis, Tim was the one who made sure doctor appointments were kept, homework was done and dinner was cooked and on the table. Larissa ruled her house and Tim having a non-confrontational personality went along with her, if for no other reason than to keep the peace. By this time she was making more than twice what Tim made. It was her money that made it possible for them to move to Clovis and buy a much larger home than the one they had in Fresno. It looked like they had it all...but did they?

By this time Kristen was a teenager and as with most teens there was attitude. Kristen fought with her mother at almost every turn. She stood up to Larissa in such a way that she felt she had no other option than to send her daughter to her parents in Clarence, Missouri. Tim was upset that his wife didn't even discuss this move with him; she'd decided this IS what will happen. And soon his beloved little girl was gone. But still Tim kept quiet.

The Schuster's entered into a bitter, rancorous separation in 2002, after nearly 20 years of marriage and two children. They tried living in the same house after the separation. However Larissa was not happy with this arrangement. From the very beginning she didn't want Tim to have anything to do with Tyler, no visitation and no kind of a relationship with his son at all. This was not okay with Tim. On more than one occasion she made the statement that she wished Tim would just die.

In late June or early July Larissa took Tyler and went on a trip out of state. Tim took this opportunity to secure a condo and move out of the family's home. Larissa was livid that he would have the nerve to leave while she was away and accused him of taking things from the house that didn't belong to him. What earlier seemed like idle threats became something more, she told a neighbor that she should just get it over with and kill Tim herself.

A Plan started formulating shortly after Tim moved out of the Clovis family home. Larissa asked James Fagone a lab assistant and Larissa's sometimes babysitter, sometimes whipping boy if he would help break in to Tim's house and help her get back somethings he took when he moved out. She felt he wasn't entitled to them and left messages on his answering machine telling him he'd better bring them back...or else.

After returning from a trip Tim came home to a house that had been burglarized and ransacked. One of the things missing...the very set of mixing bowls Larissa had had such a fit over. Who was her accomplice in the break-in...none other than James Fagone? Larissa wasn't shy about what they had done, she told her manicurist Terri Lopez, that after the break-in she would go back to Tim's house and sit in a chair and look around at what they had done. She also told Tami Belshay that "it gave her a feeling that was better than sex."

After the burglary the Schuster's relationship went even further downhill. Tim knew who had broken into his condo. Larissa's bitterness not only let her destroy things in the condo, but she even bragged about keying his truck. She said it made her happy every time she saw the marks on his truck. Tim seemed worried about what his estranged wife was capable of. He moved again, this time to a house in Clovis that had motion sensors and an alarm. He obtained a handgun and a permit to carry a concealed weapon. Larissa had told her manicurist Ms. Lopez that she prayed every night that Tim would just die. At one point Larissa told her that she could kill Tim and get away with it. She also asked one of the employees at CCRL if her boyfriend knew anyone that would kill Tim or at least rough him up. She'd made remarks like this before and all who heard them thought she was just venting because the divorce wasn't going the way she wanted it to. She said she would do anything to keep Tim from getting the business.

According to Bob and Mary Solis, Larissa would belittle and embarrass Tim in front friends and family alike. She seemed to relish the power she had over him.

In late June St Agnes let everyone know that there would be a round of layoffs coming and to be expecting it. Tim and his friend Mary Solis was on the short list to be let go. Larissa laughed when she heard the news. On July 9th Tim, Mary, her husband Bob and another friend Victor Uribe all had dinner together. The group broke up about 10pm that night, before Tim left the Solis' they had made arrangements to meet for breakfast the next morning. Tim never showed for his exit meeting or for breakfast. This worried Bob and Mary, it seems Tim was never late for anything, and if he thought he was going to be late he called. He was also supposed to pick up Tyler that evening.

His friends tried to reach Tim, calling his cell phone. Finally they called Uribe and told him that they couldn't reach Tim and would he go by the house and check on their friend. Uribe arrived at Tim's house and went inside. There didn't seem to be anything out of place, until he went to the bedroom. Tim's watch, wallet and cell phone were lying on the dresser. Uribe was now worried as well. Victor said "He never went anywhere without his cell, he kept it with him at all times, in case the kids needed him."

No one knew what had happened to Tim. The police refused to even take a missing person's report until he'd been missing 24 hours. July 10th when Tim had not been heard from in the allotted time Bob Solis filed the missing person's report. Officer John Willow from the Clovis Police Department responded to the call.

Willow found Tim's handgun under a cushion of a chair. He found Tim's cell phone in the bedroom and called all the numbers in his contacts to see if any of them had seen or heard from Mr. Schuster. When he called Larissa she said she hadn't heard from him either. He also talked to Terri Lopez and she relayed to Willow that the Schuster's were going through a rather nasty divorce. John Willow decided to turn the case over to Detectives Larry Kirkhart and Vincent Weibert.

When they entered Tim's home they noted some damage on the wall behind the chair where the gun was found earlier. They found a briefcase in the same room as the chair. Inside they found a microcassette recorder and tape. In the bedroom they found an answering machine that showed only one number, a cell phone number belonging to Larissa Schuster. Detective Kirkhart then asked Larissa to come to the police station for a chat about her missing husband.

During her interview with the detectives she told them that she and Tim were getting a divorce and that they did not communicate very well with each other. They asked her about her cell number being on the caller ID. She fabricated a story about being asleep on her couch and waking up to find she had pushed some buttons and maybe she had speed dialed Tim. They asked her if she had her phone with her and she said no. Kirkhart called for a pause in the interview and went to the parking lot to find Larissa's car. He looked in the window and saw a phone on the center console, dialed her number and the phone in the car rang.

Kirkhart went back to the interview room and asked Larissa to come with them to unlock her car and retrieve her phone. Back inside the station the interview resumed. The detective went through her contacts that she had on speed dial, none of them were Tim's number.

Larissa's whole demeanor changed, she was shaking and in the opinion of the detectives showing signs of deceit. She came clean and admitted that she had lied to the detectives and she knew she shouldn't have. She claimed she wasn't trying to be deceitful. None the less they let Schuster go home, for now. At this point in their investigation they still had no idea what had happened to Tim. Kirkhart had asked Larissa if she thought that Tim could just cash out some money and leave town, go camping or to Vegas to just get away. She told them she didn't think he would do that, that he wouldn't leave his son like that. This was still just a missing person case and most of Tim's friends thought that perhaps he had just had enough, the divorce, the custody battle, losing his job was to much for him to handle. Tami Belshay, Bob and Mary Solis and Victor

Uribe were among those friends. The detectives were thinking the same thing at this point.

With no solid leads on Tim's whereabouts detectives Weibert and Kirkhart kept searching for some clue, however small that might give them some direction on finding Tim. Kirkhart was going through Tim's ledger provided to them by Larissa. And they came across a name they were familiar with...James Fagone. They knew his name because he was the one suspected of breaking into Tim's house with Larissa shortly after Tim moved out of the family home a year earlier. They also knew that he was an associate of sorts of Larissa's.

The following Monday Detectives Kirkhart and Daly called Fagone to come and talk with them. Vince Weibert thought that perhaps Fagone might have some "inside" information on Tim's disappearance.

It seems that Fagone was a babysitter for the Schuster's son Tyler, before and after their separation. James was a good kid according to his attorney Peter Jones. "He's an above average student, higher than a 4.0 grade point average...a gentle spirit."

Fagone was nervous during the police interview. He admitted that Larissa had him help her break into Tim's house and take back things that she didn't want him to have.

James told the detectives that Larissa was going around the house looking for things and he just wanted to get the TV and some other stuff so he wasn't paying attention to what she was doing. Obviously James was scared out of his mind by now, but they pressed him more telling him they "knew he was involved somehow" with Tim's disappearance. Fagone's determination not to tell what had happened, what him and Larissa Schuster had done crumbled.

Fagone confessed that he had been there the night that Tim went missing, that he had gone to his house with a weapon. James relayed to them that Larissa had paid him the $2000 to purchase a stun gun and that he could just keep the rest for himself.

So as the day wore on James conveyed the sordid details of the night in questions.

On the night that Tim lost his job at St Agnes and had dinner with a group of friends, James had done what he was told to do by Larissa, buy a stun gun. Later he would get the call from her (Larissa). She picked him up and went to Tim's house. James laid in wait in the darkness just outside of his door. He could hear Larissa on the phone telling Tim that Tyler wasn't feeling well and she needed him to come to the front door.

A few moments later Tim opened the front door and James sprung from the shadows and attacked him wrestling him to the ground. Tim was struggling; James was using the stun gun on him, on the arm at first, not sure where else he might have zapped him. Soon Tim stopped struggling and when James looked up he saw Larissa with a rag that had been soaked in chloroform.

Were the detectives hearing this right? Was Fagone confessing to the murder of Timothy Schuster? But if they were going to believe any of it they needed some kind of evidence. They asked about the stun gun again, and what had Fagone done with it. He told them he threw it in a portable toilet on the edge of town. The investigators found the stun gun, right where James told them it should be.

Now at the same time Fagone was being interviewed Clovis Police Department got a call from a woman saying that her boss ask her to do something that in retrospect seemed a little off, suspicious even. Her Boss...Larissa Schuster. Leslie Dodd had been instructed to rent a moving truck by her boss. She was told to use her personal credit card and rent it in her own name not her boss's. A year earlier Larissa had asked the same employee to rent a storage unit near Schuster's lab, again to do it in the employees name and with her personal credit card.

Jim Koch got the call to check it out. He went to the storage unit and walked down the hall. He had been told to look for a blue barrel. When he found Schuster's unit and opened the door "there was a very very strong odor." Koch said. "I had on a breathing apparatus and gloves."

He saw the blue barrel, he opened it.

Koch said in an interview, "And when I opened the barrel I—I saw something that was very, very shocking to me and I recognized immediately as human remains. There was a barrel that's over 3/4 of the way full of fluid and portions of—of—body protruding from the fluid. And the body was obviously decaying. It was placed in acid. And the acid was basically eating away at the body."

Had Larissa Schuster killed her husband and put him in the barrel? According to James Fagone, yes she had, and he had helped her and then watched as she poured a caustic solution in on top of Tim. Worst of all, Tim was probably still alive when the acid was poured on him and he was sealed inside the barrel.

Tim had been found, the truth had come out and the Clovis detectives were on their way to Missouri to arrest Larissa for the murder of her husband Tim. They met her at the airport where she had gone to see her family. According to the detectives that arrested her for the murder she didn't even ask what had happened to Tim or how he died.

Both James Fagone and Larissa Schuster were arrested and charged with 1st degree murder.

Now that the perpetrators of Tim Schuster's murder had been arrested it was time to take them to trial. The murder was committed in the early morning hours of July 10, 2003. There was a lot left to do before the trial could begin.

The Clovis police department had to finish gathering evidence, talk to friends and family to make sure that everything was done correctly. They wanted to make sure that Larissa and James would not be let go on a technicality.

The judge had to decide if he would make this a death penalty case or a life in prison without parole case. That would be decided later. The prosecutor had to prepare a rock solid case and present the evidence to a jury in a manner that would guarantee a conviction. The defense would also be talking to people on behalf of their clients. Find people that had nothing but good things to say about them in hopes of offsetting the horrible truths that would come out at trial.

The judge separated the cases and James and Larissa would be tried separately. James was tried first. His attorney portrayed James as a misguided man who hero worshipped Larissa.

He was found guilty and is now serving a life without parole sentence.

There was so much media coverage on Larissa that the defense asked and received a change of venue. Her trial was moved to Los Angeles.

Monday October 22, 2007 Larissa's trial started. Prosecutor Dennis Peterson relayed to the jury of 9 women and 3 men just how the murder went down. He told them that Tim was still alive when the acid was poured over him while he laid head first inside the blue barrel. Her motive? She didn't want to share anything that they built during their 19 ½ years of marriage. She felt Tim didn't deserve any part of the business, or home and didn't want him to have contact with their tween son, Tyler.

CCRL employees would also testify to the facts of the blue barrel being at the lab and the day Tim was reported missing went to look for it and it was gone. They also said that Larissa had said that she should just shove Tim in the barrel and get rid of him.

A large amount of Hydrochloric acid, 12 gallons and Sulfuric acid, 4 gallons was ordered for Schuster's lab, more than ever before. Leslie Dodd (nee Fichera) testified that, "that was more acid than the lab would use in a year."

Joseph Boatwright thought Larissa was joking when she asked "if he thought a body would fit in the blue barrel."

Juror's watched several hours of Larissa's police interview. She made Tim out to be controlling and having a volatile temper. After seeing that part of the interview Bob Solis testified to the contrary, that Tim was very calm and a non-violent, non-confrontational person.

In another part of the interview with Clovis Detectives Schuster stated that "she prayed that Tim would get over this hostility about the divorce." Her manicurist Terri Lopez told a different story. Lopez said that "she told me she prayed every night he would die."

A hair stylist Becky Holland sometimes did Larissa's hair. During those appointments Larissa would rant about Tim. Holland didn't think much about it because she knew they were going through a divorce. Later though she said the hateful remarks escalated, Holland told the court, "this is getting a little creepy. It was so intense."

The jurors got to hear just how intense it was when they got to hear message after message of Larissa calling her husband awful names and making threats about their children. The prosecutor used these recordings to make a point to the jury; Larissa was in a "murderous rage". Nuttall interjected that these messages were left on Tim's machine 7 months before the murder.

And with this the prosecution rested, hoping that they had proved their case. There was one witness that they really needed to be able to lockdown the case against Schuster, they needed James Fagone. The judge had barred his confession so the jury would never hear in his own words what happened July 10, 2003. But he refused to cooperate with Peterson because he had already filed his appeal. The only thing that might have helped Peterson is the fact that James Fagone had already been convicted of Tim's murder.

Nuttall began the defense's case by telling the jury that neither he nor his client could tell them what had happened to Tim because "we don't know". And since the jury heard nearly nothing about Fagone, Roger Nuttall blamed the murder on him. After all Fagone had already been found guilty of the murder Larissa was now on trial for. Nuttall said in his opening statements that "Tim was an angry man who belittled Larissa in over-compensation for his own failings as a husband and father." And that "he began stalking Larissa after the divorce proceedings started."

Now Defense attorney Nuttall brought in a stream of witnesses that would steer the blame away from his client.

He had a medical expert that said the victim's body was cut in half and that the police had completely missed a second crime scene and the evidence from there would have proved that Fagone and others were responsible for Tim's murder not Larissa.

Nuttall even had psychiatrist Stephen Estner on the stand. Estner said that, "My impression was that Mrs. Schuster was a very direct and assertive person, and Mr. Schuster was a more passive and nurturing personality. And I think they started butting heads over that."

Larissa Schuster took the stand in her own defense and adamantly denied the charges saying, "No, I did not kill my husband." Again James Fagone would have the whole murder put squarely on him. Schuster told the jury, ""I heard him say something like 'there had been an accident and Tim is dead.' I thought he was joking."

She said that the $2000 payment to Fagone was for babysitting Tyler and housesitting while she was away on vacation with her son. Schuster said the large amount of acid was for cleaning a large scale of lab glass. Schuster seemed to explain everything away poking holes in the prosecutor's case. Would it be enough to get an acquittal? Had she actually swayed the jury?

It seemed that the trial was plagued with problems, including accusations of juror misconduct. At least one juror was replaced by an alternate due to disruptive behavior. Another admonished for giving Larissa a 'thumbs up' after her testimony. And yet with all of that...it was time for the jury to deliberate of the weeks of testimony they'd heard.

It took a little more than two days for the jury to decide on a verdict.

Guilty of Murder with a special circumstance of financial gain. The verdict came exactly one year after Fagone's.

Roger Nuttall slowed the sentencing of Larissa Schuster while he tried to find reasons to ask for a new trial. He even used the argument that there may have been juror misconduct. Nuttall wanted to talk to the jurors but Ellison said no. Nuttall appealed and the District court of Appeals told Ellison to contact the jurors on Schuster's behalf. All the jurors and alternates refused to speak to her attorney.

So on May 8, 2008, five months after being found guilty of her estranged husband's murder Larissa Leeann Schuster was sentenced to life in prison without the possibility of parole. Judge Ellison also denied her request for a new trial.

At the sentencing a total of seven people stood up to make statements about how they had been affected by the murder of Timothy Allen Schuster.

Kristen, Tim and Larissa's oldest child and only daughter made an emotionally charged statement to and about her mother.

She called her mother a demon for "taking my father away." And told her. "I pray you're continually haunted at night by the sight and sound of my father fighting for his last breathing moments on this earth. I hope you toss and turn and have horrible nightmares visualizing the horrific act of violence you have committed. Maybe later in life I can learn to forgive you, but I doubt it. This is goodbye, not just for now, but forever. This is goodbye as your daughter."

Kristen was so devastated over her father's murder she reached out to a support group murdervictims.com. Several people shared their own experiences of losing a parent at a young age hoping she could find at least a little peace.

ALICIA SHAYNE LOVERA

The life of Alicia Shayne Lovera looked like something out of a soap opera.

Born into poverty, she was ushered into a life of wealth and privilege when her mother married a rich president of a bank. She grew up to be beautiful, popular and spoiled. But she soon find herself in financial ruin when her stepfather committed suicide, leaving the family with nothing.

Her sense of entitlement still intact, she married a struggling math teacher who couldn't resist her charms.

But when the marriage became an inconvenience, she did what all black widows do.

She killed her husband.

This is her story.

EARLY LIFE

Alicia Shayne Good was born in 1966 to teenage parents. Going by her middle name Shayne, her early life wasn't easy as her parents lacked the necessary resources to provide. Her mother would divorce her father. But when Shayne turned seven-years old things to a turn for the better.

"Her mother and she were poor," journalist Jamie Satterfield said. "Her mother met Brent Mills who was a bank president and they married into that family and Brent adopted Shayne."

The change in life circumstance was jarring to the young Shayne. She was instantly given an upgrade in lifestyle as she the world was now her oyster. There were expensive vacations, cars and garish parties.

Her new stepfather, Brent Mills, was a bank executive who treated Alicia and her mother Sandy to all the spoils his job could bring. He was well regarded in the business community and had several contacts.

But Brent had inherited the bank built by his father and lacked his business acumen. He was lenient in granting loans and the bank soon grew insolvent. He was also suspected of using the bank as a money laundering service for drug dealers.

On the surface, Brent told the family that the allegations were all fraudulent. He gave them every assurance that everything would be okay.

Then he killed himself.

"He took a gun to his head and blew his brains out," forensic psychologist Paula Orange said. "That left an indelible image on Shayne's outlook on life."

His suicide would leave the family in financial ruin. The papers would ridicule Mills, giving voice to all of the wild allegations of his mismanagement. The family would be left shamed and with nothing.

The effect was devastating on Shayne. She would go from being the richest girl in the school to being dirt poor.

Again.

Shayne just wanted to get away. She had entertained aspirations of being broadcast anchor, thinking that her beauty and speaking skills would lead to an easy gig. So she decided to move out of state for college. She would attend a university in Missouri where she would meet Kelly Lovera.

They would marry a year later.

The couple would have two children over the next five years despite being the polar opposites temperamentally.

Kelly was cool, calm and wanted a quiet life. He didn't embrace the partying lifestyle that Shayne wanted.

"Theirs was a union that is hard to comprehend," Orange said. "Kelly was not en route to becoming the next bank president. He was a twenty-year old student who was struggling. He wanted to be a math teacher. Shayne wanted to live a hedonistic lifestyle. She wanted to party and spend lavishly. Why they would get married defies explanation."

Bored in Missouri, Shayne would then convince Kelly to move back to her hometown in Tennessee. Kelly would consent to the move.

A RETURN TO POVERTY

The couple would live in Sevierville which was thirteen miles north of her former luxury home in Gatlinburg. But it was light years away in terms of affluence as they were forced to rent out a small, one story townhouse.

The neighborhood they lived in was called "Frog Alley".

"A luxury once experienced becomes a necessity," Orange said. "Shayne had gotten used to living the high life. But married life, particularly one with of a lack of resources, would prove to be difficult for her."

"Frog Alley was a place for the working poor," Satterfield said. "To come back and live there would be extremely embarrassing for her."

Kelly's focus was not on making money. He was working on his master's degree in mathematics while he took a teaching position at Pellissippi College in Knoxville. Shayne would work various odd jobs to help the family make ends meet and was not happy about that.

"She had wild ambitions to become a news anchor," Orange said. "But she didn't do anything to make that happen. She wanted someone else to do all the work for her just like she experienced when her step-father financed her life."

BOREDOM SETS IN

Shayne entertained neighbors for barbecues and poker nights. The problem is, the only people that seemed to come around were other men.

She was thoroughly bored with her marriage and began to have multiple affairs.

"She would flirt with men in full view of the children," Orange said. "Men would come over ostensibly to play cards. She would play 'footsie' with them underneath the poker table. She didn't want to be a mother and got bored with that act. She wanted to party, to be the rich wild girl that she was as a teenager. The idea of staying home with a boring math teacher and two needy children was anathema to her. She wanted a way out."

The affairs would occur in her apartment when Kelly was away. Different men would come and go at various hours.

"He's (Kelly) cramping my style," Shayne told one of her lovers. "And you're so much better than him."

"Thanks," her lover said with a grin.

"Do you know anything about how to poison someone?"

"Excuse me?"

"You know," Shayne said. "How certain poisons are undetectable."

Shayne would test the waters with her lovers. She would ask them about poisons in a joking manner. But then they would soon realize that she was serious. There was an ulterior motive to her affairs.

She wanted to find someone to kill her husband.

And she would find a willing assassin in Brett Rae.

THE NEXT DOOR NEIGHBOR

Brett was young and inexperienced with women. He had never encountered anyone like the sexy Shayne Lovera.

"Brett fell very hard for Shayne," Satterfield said. "Their affair started very quickly. And it was hot and heavy."

"Brett was a rich kid," Satterfield said. "His father was a newspaper publisher (Rick Rae, a Canadian publisher of the Sevier County newspaper). He was a well-to-do guy. He was just wild. He was just one of those people who was 'full-on' all of the time. He was up for anything."

And he was completely infatuated with Shayne.

Shayne set up Brett the same way she set up her other lovers. After a torrid session of lovemaking, she popped the question.

Will you kill my husband?

"I'll do anything for you," he told her with baited breath.

Shayne offered him a deal.

"If he were to get rid of Kelly," Satterfield said. "Then he would get her. That's what Brett wanted."

"Brett let his little head do the thinking for his big head," Orange said. "He was going to inherit money from his father so he had absolutely nothing to gain by killing Shayne's husband. Nothing except sex which of course if he had money, he would have more options than a narcissistic married woman. He simply did not have the life experience to see Shayne for what she was."

She would have a party on November 5th, 1994, an outdoor barbecue with gambling and drinking. Kelly left the party early and went to sleep on the couch.

Brett would be the last one to leave that evening. On his way out the door, they both noticed Kelly asleep on the couch.

"It was a spontaneous thing," Orange said. "They didn't have a murder weapon so they used whatever was immediately available. That would be the baseball bat of Kelly's son."

Kelly would then be bludgeoned to death.

"The plan was to put him in his own vehicle," Satterfield said. "And make it look like an accident."

Brett then dragged Kelly into his jeep and drove down Highway 14. He parked near an embankment and pushed the jeep down the side, watching it carom into a tree.

He then called one of his friends to pick him up.

Brett did not keep the news of the murder to himself. He would brag to two of his friends of what he had done.

"I put him (Kelly) over a hundred foot embankment," Brett said. "I fucked his wife and killed his ass. She told me I'd get more sex and more money if I get rid of him so I did."

Brett told his friends of the other methods he thought of using to kill Kelly but that he decided to beat him to death with the baseball bat then "stage a car crash."

FINDING THE BODY

A pair of tourists would discover Kelly's black jeep below the road. Inside, they would see his bloodied dead body. Initially, they believed that he was the victim of an accident. They called the authorities and reported that it appeared as if his jeep had gone off the road and hit a tree

Park Ranger Jerry Grubb was notified of the "accident" at the Great Smoky Mountains National Park.

The whole scene, however, looked suspicious from the get-go.

"Just wasn't any skid marks," Grubb said. "No disturbed gravel. There just wasn't any disturbance in that area."

Grubb looked inside the jeep and found the body of Kelly Lovera, laying in a pool of blood trailing toward the front seat. The blood should have been trailing behind the victim if he had, in fact, struck the tree head on.

Additionally, Kelly's injuries were not consistent with a car crash victim. The facial injuries appeared to be the result of a beating, not the impact of the jeep against the tree.

MURDER ON THEIR HANDS

The autopsy would reveal that Kelly had been beaten to death and a homicide investigation ensued. Authorities would then visit Shayne's apartment and inform her of her husband's death.

She would go into hysterics, sobbing uncontrollably.

"Do you know why anyone would want to do this to him?" an investigator asked.

"He doesn't have any enemies!" she bawled.

But an officer would notice blood splatter on the glass of Kelly's diploma that was placed on a wall near the couch. They would obtain a search warrant and a crime team would arrive, spraying luminol over the apartment.

Luminol lightens up blood stains when a fluorescent ray is scanned over it.

"The whole living room lit up like a Christmas tree," Orange said. "That is when they knew they had the guilty party."

Detectives then began to question neighbors who all pointed their fingers at Brett Rae, the lover of Shayne.

Both Shayne and Brett were arrested and charged with first-degree premeditated murder.

Brett would confess quickly. He admitted to using the baseball bat and then staging the car wreck. He would be represented by Robert Ritchie who would prep him for the murder trial for nearly three months. Ritchie, however, would notice that Brett was completely obsessed with Shayne. He then turned the case over to Robert Ogle but two weeks before the trial Alan Feltes was brought in as Brett was given joint representation.

"His attorneys were flabbergasted at his refusal to give up Shayne," Orange said. "He was truly in love with her and wanted to protect her even if it meant incriminating himself."

"I did it," Brett insisted. "Just leave her out of it."

Feltes told Brett that there was no way he could win the case with all of the evidence stacked against him. The only thing Brett cared about was putting Shayne in jeopardy.

THE TRIAL

Park Ranger Jerry Grubb would testify against the killing duo, presenting the forensic evidence found at the home and jeep. Friends and family would testify that both Shayne and Brett had bragged to them about what they had done.

Going in desperation mode, Shayne would then take the stand. She wanted to tell her version of what happened that night.

"Brett had stopped by to talk to me when Kelly came out and confronted him," Shayne said. "They began fighting and Brett picked up a baseball bat. He swung it only to keep Kelly away. But then he accidentally hit him and killed him."

Shayne would go on to say that she didn't witness any of this. She was asleep and really knew nothing that happened.

"Brett and I were not lovers," Shayne said. "We were nothing more than neighbors. It was a case of fatal attraction. He had a thing for me and wanted to kill my husband."

She didn't know, however, that when both she and Brett were released on bail they were followed by a Siever County Sheriff. He followed them into the mountains and saw them having intercourse in the woods.

When Shayne was confronted with this evidence, she tried to regroup.

"I had sex with Brett," Shayne said. "But only because I had to. He threatened to involve me in the murder plot. My purpose in going there was trying to save what little bit of life I had left at that point."

The explanation did not go over well with the jury. It took them only an hour and a half to return with a guilty verdict.

OFF TO JAIL

On January 29th, 1996, both Shayne and Brett would be convicted of Kelly's murder. They would not be given the death penalty, however. The prosecution wanted a sentence of life without parole.

Feltes approached by the attorneys for Shayne. They stated that a plea agreement would be possible but it would have to be a package deal with Brett.

Feltes advised Brett to take the deal as the plea agreement would guarantee him a life sentence with possibility of parole. If he didn't take the deal, the odds would be that he would be facing life without parole.

"Just don't do anything to hurt Shayne," Brett said. "I want to see her."

"What?"

"I want to see her before I take the deal."

Brett would persist in wanting to see Shayne. Instead he would take the deal.

"His attorneys described him as having the saddest eyes they had ever seen in a courtroom," Orange said. "He was truly in love with Shayne. She, on the other hand, threw him under the bus. She was willing to say whatever it took to get herself off and it backfired."

THE AFTERMATH

Kelly's children would be placed into the care of his parents. Brett and Shayne would receive life with parole after twenty-five years.

Brett would later try to appeal his sentencing despite agreeing to a plea bargain which barred him from doing so.

His claim would be rejected.

Ray would write that "his trial was ineffective for encouraging him to accept the state's offer of life with possibility of parole; failing to prepare for mitigating circumstances at the sentencing phase; failing to properly conduct a pre-trial investigation; failing to adequately consult with him during critical stages of the proceedings; failing to advise him of his rights to direct appeal and collateral attack of his conviction; deficient performance of counsel at trial; his guilty plea was coerced and involuntary; and his conviction is void as violating the protection against double jeopardy."

"He had conceded his guilt during the guilty plea hearing and that his attorneys did the best they could...he made these admissions only because the attorneys instructed him to do so and although he agreed that he believed himself to be guilty of first degree murder at the time of his plea, he now retracts that admission."

Brett's attorney Feltes would dispute his allegations, stating that he "never had any problem with Brett being incoherent or not understanding anything he was told or advised."

Both Brett and Shayne remain in prison, waiting to be paroled in 2025.

BETTY LOU WILL KILL YOU

ALICE WILSON

Betty Lou Beets is a perfect historical example of how multifaceted crime can be, how a victim could become an aggressor, or an aggressor may adopt the mask of victimhood, and how all is not necessarily as it seems. Convicted for murdering two men and assaulting or attempting to kill four, Betty Lou's story is one that would send chills down the spine of any man from any era. Only the fourth woman to be executed for murder, despite the overall statistics hovering around forty to fifty cases of capital punishment per year, her crimes were too gruesome and cold for the court to offer her a lesser sentence... or were they? As we shall see when we delve into her history, despite Betty Lou's extensive criminal record and constant charges against her from ex husbands and her own children, the justice system was eager to give her a way out of the death sentence and allow her to live her natural life out in prison. And although there were some mitigating circumstances, it is telling that Betty Lou Beets almost got away with a life sentence in a situation where many others would have been executed without remorse.

Betty Lou Beets was born Betty Lou Dunevant on the 12th of March 1937, in Roxboro, North Carolina, USA. Her parents were initially tobacco farmers, whose main pleasure in life was alcohol, resulting in rampant alcoholism and a violent family life not atypical of the rural poor of the Great Depression. They lived on a diet of salt pork and various flours, barely touching vegetables or fruit, let alone eggs, fish, nuts or pulses, essential for developing a healthy brain and body. Furthermore, Betty Lou was disabled. She was not completely deaf, but hard of hearing due to having contracted the measles some time between the ages of three and six. Her fever was so severe and prolonged that she suffered damage to her brain and ears. As her hearing was affected at such a young age, she suffered an impairment to her speech similar to what many deaf or hard of hearing children suffer. At another time, or in another family, Betty Lou may have received treatment and hearing aids, but as a poor family in 1940, they could not afford to get her the treatment she would have needed to hear and speak normally. Her education was strongly impacted as she could not learn to read or study, resulting in borderline illiteracy and innumeracy and a frustrating life at home and away. Betty Lou also claimed she had been raped by her father in early childhood, as well as sexually abused by others. By the age of twelve her family life was falling apart. Her mother had been institutionalized due to breakdowns caused by alcoholism and Betty Lou had to drop out of school so she could care for her younger brother and sister. Her father, who seemed to see her as a surrogate mother for her siblings, became guarded against any sign of Betty Lou escaping and would beat her for not taking full responsibility for her siblings. She was often at the doctor's office or in hospital for the injuries he inflicted on her. She finally left school completely. The family moved to Hampton, Virginia, while Betty Lou was still a young girl, so that her father could work as a machinist. They were poor, she was young and disabled and she was a victim at the hands of the very people who were supposed to care for her. These circumstances were hardly the healthiest for the young girl to grow up in, and it is not shocking that Betty Lou became increasingly unstable and inclined to criminality in such an environment during such a time of deprivation. However it is also noteworthy that many more people suffered equal or worse hardship, yet did not turn to criminal activity. Perhaps it was the combination of everything, all together at once, but as she grew up something was going very, very wrong inside Betty Lou.

At the age of fifteen she married her first husband, Robert Franklin Branson. Far from an age where anyone feels quite ready to move into adulthood, Betty Lou was married for the first time. She would remain with him for seventeen years before finally divorcing. Although she levied accusations of violence against all her husbands, Robert Franklin Branson was the only one whose life she did not threaten directly herself. It appears he picked up where her father left off. If she was ever a unilateral victim, this may have been the one time. Within the first year she attempted suicide and became pregnant. They had a daughter together. She also later had a son with Robert Branson, who was also named Robert after his father. They went onto have four more children. Their children may have been a factor in reducing the marital violence, extending the duration of the relationship and, ultimately, saving Robert Branson Senior's life. In 1958 he evicted her from their home and put her on a bus to Virginia while he kept her children, at which point Betty again attempted suicide via an overdose of sleeping pills. They divorced in 1969, which left Betty Lou a financial and emotional wreck.

Being single took its toll on Betty Lou. She attached her self-worth to her ability to stay married. She began drinking to fight her feelings of loneliness.

Between her own insecurities and the hard time she had getting money from either Robert Branson or the Welfare service to support her, Betty Lou soon felt she needed to remarry. She married Billy York Lane at the age of thirty two. Their marriage was a tumultuous one, and very short. There was evidence of mutual violence and disregard for each other's wellbeing. Lane had been abusive towards a previous partner and Betty Lou responded to his violence in turn. Her daughters recall how he used to beat her senseless and how she used to attack him. He initially wanted to charge her for attempted murder, but swiftly dropped the charges after he was forced to admit he had attacked her, broken her nose and threatened her life. They divorced the same year and remarried again shortly after the trial. After Betty Lou shot at him, Billy York Lane divorced her again, only a month after their remarriage, this time for good. It would prove the wisest decision of his life, as her subsequent husbands found out.

Betty Lou remained single for a year and unmarried for eight more years. During the interim Betty Lou worked in a warehouse, then took up work at a topless bar to cover the bills. She sent two of their children back home to Branson, as she could not afford to care for them. She went on to marry Ronnie C. Threlkold, her boyfriend of seven years, at the age of forty. However this relationship would be as unpredictable, violent and dangerous for Ronnie as it was for Billy. In this case there was little evidence Ronnie had been violent towards Betty Lou, although she accused him of violence at later dates, but her habits had been firmly cemented and she continued to display abusive behaviour towards him. She also continued to work at the topless bar, resulting in arrests and thirty days in country jail under the charge of public lewdness. Despite their seven year courtship, the marriage lasted just a year, culminating in Betty Lou Beets's attempted homicide of Ronnie in 1978, where she shot him in the stomach, wounding him, and their divorce in 1979.

She married Doyle Wayne Barker at the age of forty one, closely after her divorce from Threlkold. Their marriage lasted a mere seven weeks before her violent behaviour drove Doyle away from her. However his own violence was undeniable. He had stalked her, assaulted her and raped her during their short relationship. The day he left Betty Lou had bruises all over her face, neck, arms and chest. There is no available record of the divorce, however all living parties assumed it had taken place. However Doyle Wayne did not get out of their marriage unscathed. He disappeared after their divorce and his body was found years later, buried under a garage, killed by three gunshots.

But this grisly deed was not uncovered for many more years to come. Rather, Betty Lou went on to marry a firefighter named Jimmy Don Beets, her final husband, at the age of forty four.

"Jimmy Don Beets was a wonderful man," said a family friend. "He was loved by so many people. An old country boy that a lot people had respect for."

Their courtship would last a mere six months. Betty Lou would meet Jimmy while she worked as a waitress and the seduction began. Her two sons moved in with them. This would be her final marriage, and her actions within it would be her undoing. Although their courtship had been pleasant, they both suffered from alcoholism, which slowly drove their marriage to the same violence she had experienced previously. Less than a year later she murdered him by gunshot, and this time she was caught. Robert Branson, her son from her first marriage, had been informed that she intended to kill her last husband, telling him to steer clear of the residence as the murder took place. On the 6th of August 1983, Robert Branson Junior left their home and Betty Lou Beets committed the gruesome act. Not only did Robert provide evidence that the act was premeditated, but he also was expected to participate. Two hours after leaving the house, Robert Branson Junior returned, finding his step father dead with two gunshot wounds in his body. Rather than seek assistance, Robert Branson Junior, either tainted by a lifetime with a mother who viewed abuse and murder as daily events or himself an individual with low empathy, helped his mother to dispose of the body. Betty Lou Beets and Robert Branson Junior carted Jimmy Don Beets' body outside to an ornamental wishing well that stood in the front yard of their house. Undetected, they cast the body inside.

Then, Betty Lou returned to the house to cover up her acts. She called the police to report her husband missing from their Cedar Creek Lake home. The next day, Betty Lou became more devious. Perhaps inspired, perhaps unnerved by her success killing Doyle Wayne Barker, she realized she needed to create a story with which to divert the police from her trail. Robert Branson Junior recalled to the press how she had taken some of Jimmy Don Beets's heart medication down to his boat at the lake. Then she had removed the propeller, placed the medication in the boat and abandoned it, floating loosely in the water. Later that day, as the twenty four hours since Jimmy Don Beets's initial disappearance drew to a close, various officials began the search for the presumably missing man. Officers from the Henderson County Sheriff's department, various members of the fire department, as well as agents from the Texas Parks and Wildlife department searched for three weeks. They naturally found no body. However they did find Jimmy Don Beets's boat drifting in the lake, near to the Redwood Beach Marina. There they found his fishing license, an unused life jacket and the heart medication which Betty Lou Beets had placed there. Not knowing anything about the murder or the forged evidence, they brought Betty Lou Beets to the Marina as the sole witness, where she identified the boat and its contents as those of her husband. Although no body had been recovered, it was considered case closed.

Betty Lou Beets would have likely got away with both murders, were it not for confidential information given to the Henderson County Sheriff's Department two years later. The information suggested that Jimmy Don Beets had not disappeared innocently, and that his assumed death, with no body that had been found, may be the result of foul play. The evidence was enough that the cold case was reopened in Spring 1985. As their suspicions became stronger, the investigators were drawn to Betty Lou Beets, who was arrested on the 8th of June of 1985 and then booked into the Henderson County Jail. An officer on the case, Rick Rose, who had been in charge of her arrest warrant, secured a further warrant to search the Beets's home and lands, including the yard. Ultimately, they discovered Jimmy Don Beets's remains buried under the wishing well where he had been left two years prior. But another discovery would surface that would further disturb the case. Also in the back yard was a storage shed which could be moved. When the officers moved it, something compelled them to disturb the soil that had lain there several years. Perhaps it was some confidential evidence or perhaps it was just intuition, but it paid off when they discovered a second body. Doyle Wayne Barker, still missing, was buried there, with three bullets in his body. All five bullets matched the .38 caliber pistol which had been seized from their home after another incident of Betty Lou's violent outbursts. Thanks to the calls she had made the very day of his disappearance there was no room to argue that she had been abusing drugs or alcohol at the time, but there had been no physical evidence that suggested to detectives at the time that Jimmy Don had been abusing her when the incident took place. Her position was weak.

Faced with the evidence, Robert Branson Junior and his sister Shirley finally confessed to their awareness of the killings, as well as their hand in the crimes that had taken place. Not only had Betty Lou told her son about the murder, but she had also informed her daughter, by the Shirley Stegner and not living at the family home, that she planned on killing her husband. Shirley was motivated by her confession to also confess to her involvement in another crime. She told the detectives that she had been involved in the burial of Doyle Wayne Barker's body in October of 1981 after Betty Lou had shot him to death.

In an effort to make herself more likeable to the jury, Betty Lou Beets raised her history of domestic violence as an excuse for her violent behaviour, levying charges against all her prior husbands, as well as her father. However, this would be the first that anyone had heard of most of these charges. This may have been due to attitudes of the times, a desire to protect her children, or the apparently two-sided nature of most of these incidents, however the jury would not believe her claims. They were just too convenient. Instead, it was clear to them that Betty Lou Beets was an unstable and dangerous woman and the only connection between the five men she married and their violence. Whatever the situation was, her psychological well being was never considered during the trial. Despite the obvious impact her upbringing and life would have on her mental state and the fact that her actions up until that point were indicative of definite mental illness, the trial system of the time did not account for that.

Furthermore, the premeditated nature of her actions was evident through her children's abundant testimonials, where they confessed she had shared her intent to kill not only the husbands she managed to murder, but that she had expressed a desire to kill all the men she had been married to. Not only that, but her success concealing the bodies, under the wishing well and under the garden shed, showed a lack of remorse and serious consideration of her crimes. However it seems Betty Lou had not been as careful as she thought. As soon as the trial began, various other witnesses emerged to testify against her. Various people recalled her attempting to collect life insurance of over a hundred thousand dollars as well as a pension of over a thousand dollars a month after Jimmy Don's declared death. A year after the official death of Jimmy Don Beets, she successfully sold his boat, the primary evidence that he had disappeared. She claimed she did not know about his pension or insurance, however seeing as Jimmy Don Beets was already retired and claiming his pension, this claim fell short. Furthermore, had she no awareness of them she would not have pursued either so actively. She claimed she had been told about them when she visited an attorney by the name or E. Ray Andrews about a fire insurance claim she needed to make, at which point he discovered she could claim his insurance and pension. However her own filing for these benefits did not align with the supposed visit, and the only person who could say for sure that she had not known about her deceased husband's finances was E. Ray Andrews himself, who agreed to represent her in exchange for the rights to book and movie deals concerning her life and case.

Betty Lou Beets was indicted for murder for remuneration or the promise of remuneration, with her recovery of his life insurance and pension as evidence. She plead not guilty and was taken to trial, where she was found guilty of the capital offence of first degree murder on the 11th of October of 1985. She was found again guilty during a hearing on the 14th of October 1985 and was sentenced to death by the trial court. This was due to her prior history of violence and attempted murders, which suggested that she would present a threat to others in the future, specifically to any man who entered a relationship with her again. Yet her conviction and sentence were quickly and successfully appealed to the Texas Court of Criminal Appeals. Such was the situation that, under Texas law, crime for the sake of insurance and pension claims was not covered by the definition of "murder for remuneration", instead falling into two separate categories of first degree murder and insurance fraud, or crime with intent to commit insurance fraud. The Texas Court of Criminal Appeals reversed her conviction for capital murder, citing the Texas Penal Code as evidence that her particular case could not be filed as "murder for remuneration". The State then requested a rehearing of the cause. Although her original conviction had been overturned, the fact remained that Betty Lou Beets was guilty of homicide under some circumstance or another. On the 21st of September of 1988, the Court of Criminal Appeals reinstated her conviction and sentence based on the evidence received. Betty Lou Beets was on death row. Her execution was scheduled for the 8th of November 1989.

However her court case did not go as it should have in the first place. Attorney E. Ray Andrews was heavily invested in sensationalizing her case as much as he could, seeing as he would profit enormously from the case blowing up into a media phenomenon. So although she claimed and he later agreed that she had known nothing of her husband's finances, the trial was conducted under the assumption that she was fully aware of the money she would receive. Not only that, but E. Ray Andrews did everything in his power to create a more dramatic case on both sides, which ultimately meant excluding Betty Lou from much of the information about her own trial. Betty Lou was becoming desperate at this point. Although she had a long history of domestic violence, attempted murder and two bodies in her garden, she decided to attempt to blame the murder of Jimmy Don Beets on Robert Branson Junior, her own son. She did not seem to have made the statement in sound mind, but E. Ray Andrews allowed her to speak on her own behalf and did not retract it, as it added dramatic quality to the event. He tried to cover up later, saying that Betty Lou had possibly been taking the blame for her son, however he had no proof other than that Robert Branson Junior was male and from a rough background. This statement and its acceptance horrified the court, as it was alarming to them to see a mother who, rather than protect her children, was willing to throw them under the bus by falsely accusing them of a crime she had more than evidently committed. Furthermore, by admitting and adhering to the story that Robert Branson Junior was in fact the actual killer, Betty Lou lost all chances of arguing that she acted in self-defence and made her own accusations of domestic violence against Jimmy Don and her prior husbands completely irrelevant. This is despite the fact that a leading domestic violence specialist of the time believed Betty Lou Beets had been significantly mentally impacted by her experiences, and that she suffered "the emotional, cognitive, and behavioural components of battered woman syndrome, rape trauma syndrome, and PTSD" which he added must have interacted with her pre-existing organic brain damage from her childhood illness, history of battering and substance abuse. All together, this would have presented a robust case for her mental illness and need for treatment rather than punishment. However E. Ray Andrews discarded this option in favour of the more dramatic choice of supporting Betty Lou's accusation against her son. They became stuck in the position of having to argue she did not kill her husband at all. This context may have reduced her sentence, or made her eligible to claim insanity. However neither of these options were available.

Throughout the entire case, E. Ray Andrews failed to represent her seriously and did nothing to prevent her from shooting herself in the foot repeatedly. In fact, seeing the case was a lost cause and that he stood to gain more from her sentence than her freedom, Andrews began drinking heavily for the duration of the trial. He chose not to bear witness to her claims that she did not know about Jimmy Don Beets's pension or insurance, which would have transformed the case to one of murder in the context of domestic violence, rather than murder for remuneration. He managed to offer the jury no reasons to consider that Betty Lou was not a serious threat to those around her, eventually sealing her fate. Yet he remained her attorney for the duration of her appeal as well. It was he who raised the point that her financial gain was not necessarily the motivator for murder, but a by product. He also finally raised that she was not aware of the insurance or pension until she spoke to him, however this was met with scepticism due to his negligence to mention it any sooner, and was perceived as a lie in effort to overturn Betty Lou's criminal charges after his initial failure to protect her.

On the 16th of October 1989, Betty Lou filed a motion called a stay of execution which would delay her execution to give her time to prepare and file a habeas corpus application with the state. On the 1st of November she filed the application and the trial court delayed her execution so that the claims she was raising, such as consideration towards her mental state and marital conditions, could be properly addressed. During this time Betty Lou wrote several letters from prison in which she attempted to defend her good name and that of her last husband. She attempted to balance the accusations that she was a black widow by reminding the court that she was Jimmy Don's fourth wife as well. However his previous wives did not come forward to support her. She also defended her own identity, denying that she ever worked as a barmaid, regardless of her own charges for lewd behaviour, and that she was never on welfare, despite her claims after her first divorce. She also said that the Fire Department Chaplain, who stated he had informed her about Beets's insurance and pension, had spoken to her sister in law, Betty Beets, instead. She even quibbled over the descriptions of her garden, insisting the well was a planter in the shape of a well and not an actual well. It was clear that Betty Lou Beets was desperate to save face and project a more pleasant, more ordinary identity than the one which E. Ray Andrews had created for her in the courtroom. It was also clear that her mental health was degrading as she endured life in prison and submitted her habeas corpus petition. In her petition she argued against her sentence of the death penalty, raising issues such as the alleged value Jimmy Don Beets apparently added the community, the testimonials of victims and sufferers whose statements were unconstitutional under the Victim Impact Statements act of 1987, and the poor assistance which E. Ray Andrews provided, especially regarding her history of domestic abuse. Yet without his help in writing and presenting the letter, her claims were weak and not fully backed by legal evidence. Andrews did not visit her from the point of her sentencing and prepared for her trials without ever speaking to her. Furthermore, she could have claimed that his services were provided against American Bar Association rules, which prohibit the trade of legal services for copyright issues, such as the rights to her case. None of this was raised by her against him, and as such it was not considered during her habeas corpus appeal.

However on the 27th of June her appeal for state habeas corpus was turned away. She was placed in the position of proving that, had E. Ray Andrews presented a testimony about her lack of awareness of the insurance and her history of domestic violence, the jury would have judged her not guilty of a capital crime. Without a proper attorney to defend her, it would be impossible for Betty Lou to prove this was the case, and the court deemed Andrews's mistakes to have been harmless to her trial. The Fifth Circuit Court of Appeals went on to turn down her final appeals. The judges remained convinced that, regardless of any remaining evidence, Betty Lou Beets's history of violence and attempted murder, along with the two concealed bodies in her garden, were evidence enough that a death sentence was a fair response to the crime that had taken place. She had displayed violence her whole life, even towards men who had not presented a threat to her, and had attempted to kill all but one of her husbands. She had concealed her murders carefully and for many years and was willing to place the blame on her own adult son. In other words, regardless of her own situation, her criminal intent was viewed as evident and incorrigible, and her death sentence was the only fitting end to her crime spree.

On death row, Betty Lou Beets retained some supporters, mostly her own children. Some of Betty Lou's daughters went to E. Ray Andrews with photographic evidence of the domestic abuse she had suffered in order to request a parole review, but were declined. They insisted on presenting the evidence that she had suffered and that her acts of violence were a result of brain damage and abuse, not of malicious intent. Faye Lane, one of her daughters, insisted that her mother would only have done anything so horrific if she believed she was abused. Domestic violence awareness groups and charities acting against the death sentence appealed to have her sentence changed to a life sentence in prison, based not only on her own suffering, but on their universal stance against the irreversible process of the death penalty. Yet even those defending her maintained that she was a violent, unpredictable woman and not safe to exit into the general public.

And not all her children were so kind. Shirley told the press that Doyle Wayne Barker was killed because he owned the trailer where they lived, and that after the divorce which Barker had initiated, Betty Lou and her children would be evicted from the trailer and left homeless. This set a precedent where even her own daughter could not believe that Betty Lou was completely unaware of the financial benefits of murdering Jimmy Don Beets, especially not after she had successfully killed Barker. Knowing that she was still doubted and seeing hope as ever distant, Betty Lou composed her memoirs from death row, presenting her case.

Beets turned to her last resort which was to appeal to then-governor George W. Bush to spare her life. After a media incident where he jokingly insulted the last woman to be executed in Texas in an insensitive manner, George W. Bush seemed keen to prove he had no bias against women, even in the prison system, and agreed to review her case. This would have meant hearing the witnesses which had not been heard by the trial lawyer and present a case against her execution based on the circumstances of her life, including medical and psychiatric evidence. He could have granted her a thirty day reprieve in which he made his decision, however this never materialized. His number was made available and he received thousands of calls and letters from people urging him to spare her, with only fifty seven endorsing her sentence. Yet he did not grant the reprieve or halt the execution.

Betty Lou Beets was finally executed on the 24th of February of 2000, via lethal injection. Protestors from various organisations gathered outside as her sentence awaited. She declined both her last meal and her final statement, having been given by then enough time to make sense of what was happening and to say everything which needed to be said. Strapped to the death chamber gurney, she received her injection at six pm and died within eighteen minutes. She was sixty two years old. She left behind five adult children, nine grandchildren and six great-grandchildren, as well as her memoirs. Her story may be shocking, and it may be hard to pick sides at times, but that is exactly why her trial presents a solid case against the black and white ideals the court system held regarding crime and punishment, perpetrator and victim, defence and offence. Someone can at once be a victim of horrific crimes and a perpetrator of them, at once be a defendant and raise accusations, at once deserve punishment yet suffer a crime gone unpunished. There is no doubt that Betty Lou Beets was a violent woman who invited violence into her own life, an alcoholic and a murderer. However there is no doubt either that she was a good mother within her capacity, a victim of a series of horrific crimes, a disabled person with a background she could not escape and a desperate woman who saw no way out of her situation. Neither black nor white, good not bad, Betty Lou Beets sits in the grey areas of the law.

www.ingramcontent.com/pod-product-compliance
Lightning Source LLC
Chambersburg PA
CBHW031348160726
47993CB00002B/868